CRANIUM CRACKERS
BOOK 3

SERIES TITLES:
CRANIUM CRACKERS BOOK 1
CRANIUM CRACKERS BOOK 2
CRANIUM CRACKERS BOOK 3
CRANIUM CRACKERS BOOK 4

Anita Harnadek

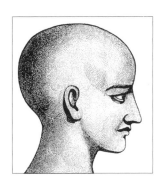

© 1997, 1991
THE CRITICAL THINKING CO.
(BRIGHT MINDS™)
www.CriticalThinking.com
P.O. Box 1610 • Seaside • CA 93955-1610
Phone 800-458-4849 • FAX 831-393-3277
ISBN 0-89455-666-5
Printed in the United States of America

Table of Contents

Add & Subtract
Clock arithmetic 69–82

Add, Subtract & Multiply
Other bases 89–97

Addition
CrossNumber™ Puzzles 17–21
Replace the letters 134

Analogies
Analogies in proportions 152–75
Identifying analogous relationships 31–7
Rearranging analogies 40–6
Reasoning by analogy 47–50
Stating analogies in standard form 38–9

Analogy preparation
Finding common attributes 29
Identifying synonyms 27–8
Identifying the outsider 30

Clock arithmetic 69–82

Diophantine problems 67, 129, 148, 178

Fractions
Analogies in proportions 152–75
Index of refraction 115
Miscellaneous problems 132–3, 143, 150

Glossary 215–6

Index 217

Index of refraction 115

Indirect proof problems 159–75

Logic
Counterexamples 8–16, 73–4
Drawing inferences 7, 22–6, 63, 85, 118, 142, 147, 149, 176
Fantasy or true to life? 3–6
Indirect proof 159–75
Math Mind Benders® 123–8
Mind Benders® 138–41
Miscellaneous problems 144
Truth-tellers and liars 1–2
Water jugs problems 68, 84, 130–1, 151
Weighing balls 100, 179

Mixed operations
Math Mind Benders® 123–8
Operators and order of precedence 51–61

Number patterns 108–10

Order of operations 51–61

Other bases 89–97

Puzzles
CrossNumber™ Puzzles 17–21
Math Mind Benders® 123–8
Rearrange letters 66, 83, 98, 116, 136, 177
Replace the letters 134

Raising to a power
Math Mind Benders® 124
Operators and order of precedence 51–61

Teaching Suggestions/Answers
Answers and Comments 183–213
Arithmetic Levels of This Series 182
General Information 181–2
Introduction 181
References 182–3
Teaching Thinking 183

Verbal reasoning problems
Finding common attributes 29
Following directions 62, 117
Identifying analogous relationships 31–7
Identifying synonyms 27–8
Identifying the outsider 30
Rearranging analogies 40–6
Reasoning by analogy 47–50
Relevant information 101–7
Stating analogies in standard form 38–9

Word problems
Diophantine problems 67, 129, 148, 178
Miscellaneous problems 64–5, 86–8, 99, 119–22, 132–3, 135, 137, 143–6, 150
Rearrange letters 66, 83, 98, 116, 136, 177
Speed of light 111–5

Reference

Basic Thinking Skills

FANTASY OR TRUE TO LIFE?

DIRECTIONS

A few statements are given to start a story.

Accept these statements as true.

These statements are followed by some lettered statements.

Decide whether the lettered statements sound true to life or whether they sound more like fantasy.

EXAMPLE

Problem:

Diane had a very intelligent cat named Tiger. Diane taught Tiger to walk for a short distance on his hind legs. She also taught him to sit up and to shake hands.

a. Tiger could tell from the way Diane acted that she disliked his sharpening his claws on the furniture, so he stopped doing that and instead sharpened his claws on a tree when Diane let him go outside. *true*

b. Tiger got bored with playing with a ball of string, so he found Diane's crochet hook and crocheted a small doily from the string. *fantasy*

Answers:

a. true to life

b. fantasy

PROBLEMS

4. Hilde was exceptionally good at solving jigsaw puzzles, and she en-joyed the challenge presented by each new puzzle.

    Sometimes she took two puzzles apart and mixed all the pieces together and then assembled the puzzles again.

    One day she mixed up all the pieces of

    a. two 500-piece puzzles and had both puzzles reassembled in four hours *true.*

    b. two 1000-piece puzzles and had both puzzles reassembled in four hours *Fantasy. (She'd have to be a genius)*

    c. two 500-piece puzzles, and then she turned all of the pieces over so that the picture side of each piece was facing downward and couldn't be seen. She had both puzzles reassembled in five hours without turning any of the pieces over so that the picture side was up *True, If she had them memorized. Fantasy, otherwise*

Reference

*Basic
Thinking
Skills*

5. Laura didn't understand today's arithmetic lesson.

The teacher had already said what they were going to study tomorrow, and Laura didn't see how she could understand that if she didn't understand today's lesson, so she

   a. stayed after school to get extra help from the teacher, and then she understood the lesson *true*

   b. asked her big brother for help with it, but she still didn't understand the lesson when he was through explaining it to her

true

   c. told her dog, King, about it and showed him her arithmetic book. King read the material and then explained it to Laura so that she understood it *fantasy*

Reference

*Basic
Thinking
Skills*

d. said, "Oh, I wish some good angel would appear and explain it to me!" A good angel appeared and explained it to her, and Laura understood the lesson

fantasy

e. said, "Oh, I wish I had a fairy godmother who'd make me smart enough to understand this!" But no fairy godmother appeared, and Laura still didn't understand the lesson when she went back to school the next day *true*

f. gave up trying to understand it. She picked numbers out of thin air for the answers to the fifteen homework problems, and when the homework was checked in class the next day, every one of Laura's answers turned out to be right *fantasy, or dumb luck*

g. concentrated very hard the next day on the new lesson, and she understood every bit of it, even though she still didn't understand the previous lesson, and even though the new lesson was based on the previous lesson *it is possibly true*

DRAWING INFERENCES

DIRECTIONS

Sometimes a problem needs only a "yes" or "no" answer, but be ready to tell why you chose your answer if you are asked about it.

Sometimes a problem doesn't tell you enough to let you know for sure what the answer is. In this case, answer "not enough information."

PROBLEMS

6. There are three apartment houses in a row: Tall Towers, Royal Crescent, and White Oaks.

   You are standing in front of one of them. Tall Towers is on your right. White Oaks is to the right of Tall Towers.

   Where are you standing?

7. If there are 36 zaffirs in a dineb, then how many zaffirs are in 2 dinebs?

8. Linda likes beef stew better than roast beef.
   Lindy likes roast beef better than hamburger.

   Can Linda and Lindy be the same person?

Reference

Critical Thinking Books 1 & 2

COUNTEREXAMPLES

LESSON

Some statements are false but cannot be proved false. For example, suppose I told you that I've always wanted a zebra. I haven't, but there is no way for you to prove that I lied to you.

Other statements are false and *can* be proved false. For instance, suppose I said that everyone wants a zebra. My words will be proved false if you find one person who does *not* want a zebra. That one person will be a *counterexample* to my statement.

A counterexample to a statement is a *specific* example that proves the statement is false.

EXAMPLE

Statement: Every dog is green.

These are counterexamples:

My dog is pink.

My sister's dog isn't green.

Mr. MacDonald's dog is orange with black spots.

These are not counterexamples:

I don't believe that. (No example is given.)

No dog is green. (No example is given.)

My cat is black. (This doesn't make the statement false.)

No bulldog is green. (This proves the statement false, but it is not a counterexample because it is not a *specific* example.)

Only certain kinds of statements can have counterexamples to them. (The next lesson will say more about this.) For these kinds of statements, counterexamples are nearly always the easiest way to prove the statements are not true.

Reference

*Critical
Thinking
Books 1
& 2*

DIRECTIONS

A statement is given and is followed by several lettered sentences.

Tell whether or not each lettered sentence is a counterexample to the statement, and tell why.

PROBLEM

9. Statement: Every teenager should have a pet. (Assume that the people named below are teenagers.)

    a. A lot of teenagers don't have pets.

    b. Marty and his parents live in an apartment, and their landlord won't let them keep any.

    c. Not every teenager wants a pet.

    d. Some teenagers are allergic to animals.

    e. Sam's parents are poor, and he goes to work before and after school every day, so he doesn't have time to be with a pet or to take care of one.

    f. Moira doesn't like dogs or cats.

    g. Luke doesn't want a pet, and anyone who doesn't want a pet shouldn't have one.

Reference

Critical Thinking Books 1 & 2

LESSON CONT.

A counterexample contradicts a statement about everything of a kind. This means that only certain kinds of statements can have counterexamples.

These statements are about everything of a kind. There may be counterexamples to these statements.

> All dogs are green.
>
> No dog is green.
>
> If something is a dog, then it is green.

No single example will prove any of these next statements false because the statements are not about everything of a kind. Such statements can have no counterexamples.

> Some dogs are green.
>
> Many dogs are green.
>
> Only a few dogs are green.

Notice that a counterexample to a statement proves that the statement is false in one case, but it doesn't prove the statement is false in every case.

In other words, a counterexample simply shows that the statement should not have been made about *everything*.

EXAMPLE

> Statement: All dogs are green.
>
> Counterexample: My dog isn't green.
>
> The counterexample proves the statement false, but it doesn't prove that no dog is green.

Reference

Critical Thinking Books 1 & 2

DIRECTIONS

Tell whether or not each lettered statement is the kind of statement for which a counterexample might be found.

In other words, tell whether or not the statement could be proved false by finding just one example.

PROBLEM

10. a. Everybody should learn how to cook.

b. Professional football players are physically tough.

c. Very few TV stars are as good-looking as they seem to be on TV.

d. Nobody likes a smart aleck.

e. People almost never want to believe that teenagers are sensible people.

f. Some inventions have been a waste of time.

g. It's easier to learn from a computer than it is to learn from a person.

h. Most people like to get birthday presents.

Reference

Critical Thinking Books 1 & 2

DIRECTIONS

A statement is given and is followed by lettered sentences.

Tell whether or not each lettered sentence is a counterexample to the statement. If it is not, then tell why not.

EXAMPLE

Problem: All boys like to play baseball.

　　a.　Brad is a boy, and he doesn't like to play baseball.

　　b.　Cathy is a girl, and she likes to play baseball.

Answer: a.　Yes

　　　　　b.　No. The statement does not say anything about what girls like or don't like.

PROBLEMS

11.　When a teenager goes to a store, the clerks almost never give them the same service they give an adult.

　　a.　My cousin is fifteen, and she always gets the same courteous service that her mother gets at a store.

　　b.　The clerks at our neighborhood pharmacy don't give good service to anyone, adult or teenager.

Reference

*Critical
Thinking
Books 1
& 2*

12. Nobody expected George Washington to be elected the first president of the United States.

   a. Successful generals are always good leaders, and leadership is needed in a president.

   b. Benjamin Franklin thought that Thomas Jefferson would be elected as the first president.

   c. Paul Revere firmly supported George Washington.

13. All great chefs are men.

   a. You don't know about all great chefs, so that's an illogical thing to say.

   b. My aunt Miriam was listed in a recent poll of recognized gourmets as one of the ten best chefs in the world.

   c. Isaac's parents have lots of company at their house, and his mother always gets outstanding compliments on her cooking.

14. If a girl is a teenager, then she's good at swimming.

   a. Julian is 14 years old, and he's a terrible swimmer.

   b. Doris is a marvelous swimmer, and she's 10 years old.

Reference

Critical Thinking Books 1 & 2

15. Everybody likes a good adventure story.

  a. My mother doesn't like them unless they're westerns.

  b. My father prefers mysteries.

  c. Some people don't like them at all.

  d. I like them better than any other kind of story.

16. Nearly everyone likes to get free samples of new products.

  a. Most of the people I know don't like to get free samples. I'll give you a list of the people I know and a list of those that don't like free samples if you want actual examples.

  b. I don't like getting free samples of new kinds of sauerkraut.

Reference

Critical Thinking, Books 1 & 2

17. Suppose a statement about everything of a kind is true. Can there be a counterexample to it? If so, give an example. If not, how come?

18. Suppose you are given the statement,

"All zoffers are middigs,"

and you find a zoffer that is not a middig.

a. Have you found a counterexample to the statement?

b. Have you proved the statement false?

c. Have you proved that no zoffers are middigs?

d. Have you proved that some (at least one) zoffers are not middigs?

e. Have you proved that if anything is a zoffer, then it is not a middig?

f. Have you proved that if anything is a zoffer, then it is not necessarily a middig?

g. Have you proved that if anything is not a zoffer, then it is a middig?

h. Have you proved that if anything is a middig, then it is not a zoffer?

i. Have you proved that some (at least one) middigs are not zoffers?

Reference

*Critical
Thinking,
Books 1
& 2*

19. Suppose you are given the statement,

"All zoffers are middigs,"

and you find a middig that is not a zoffer.

a. Have you found a counterexample to the statement?

b. Have you proved the statement false?

c. Have you proved that no zoffers are middigs?

d. Have you proved that some (at least one) zoffers are not middigs?

e. Have you proved that if anything is a zoffer, then it is not a middig?

f. Have you proved that if anything is a zoffer, then it is not necessarily a middig?

g. Have you proved that if anything is not a zoffer, then it is a middig?

h. Have you proved that if anything is not a zoffer, then it is not a middig?

i. Have you proved that if anything is a middig, then it is not a zoffer?

j. Have you proved that some (at least one) middigs are not zoffers?

CROSSNUMBER™ PUZZLES

LESSON

A number *below* a diagonal shows a sum for the squares underneath. A number *above* a diagonal shows a sum the squares to the right.

You are to write any digits from 1 through 9, one digit per square, so that their sums are correct. You may use a digit more than once in the puzzle, but you may not use it more than once for any one sum.

To solve the puzzle, look for sums that will be forced. (For example, don't start with 15, because there are several ways to get a sum of 15 from three digits.)

We will start with 3, which has to be either 1 + 2 or 2 + 1. See what happens when we try 2 + 1.

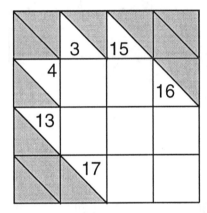

Now 4 has to be 2 + 2, but we are not allowed to use the same digit twice for a sum. So 3 has to be 1 + 2, and 4 is forced to be 1 + 3.

Reference

Cross-
Number™
Puzzles—
Sums:
Book A-1

The squares for 3 and 4 are filled in now, so we look for another sum to be forced. We choose 17, which must be either 8 + 9 or 9 + 8. If we use 9 + 8, the 8 will fall in one of 16's squares. But 16 can't be 8 + 8. So 17 has to be 8 + 9, and 16 is forced to be 7 + 9.

	3	15	
4	1	3	16
13	2		7
	17	8	9

There is only one square left to be filled in, and that digit has to be the same for both 15 and 13.

	3	15	
4	1	3	16
13	2	4	7
	17	8	9

We happened not to use any digit more than once in the puzzle, but the rules did not forbid it. The rules say only that we cannot use a digit more than once for any one sum.

Reference

*Cross-
Number™
Puzzles—
Sums:
Book A-1*

DIRECTIONS

Fill in the grid so that the digits add up to the sums shown.

- A number below a diagonal shows the sum for the squares underneath.

- A number above a diagonal shows the sum for the squares to the right.

- You may use only the digits 1 through 9 (one digit per square).

- You may not use any digit more than once to get a sum.

PROBLEM

20.

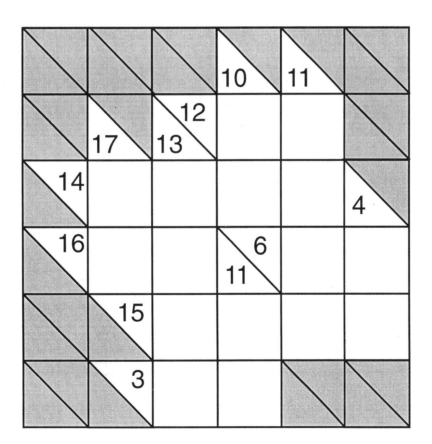

Reference

*Cross-
Number™
Puzzles—
Sums:
Book B-1*

DIRECTIONS

Fill in the grid so that the digits add up to the sums shown.

- A number below a diagonal shows the sum for the squares underneath.

- A number above a diagonal shows the sum for the squares to the right.

- You may use only the digits 1 through 9 (one digit per square).

- You may not use any digit more than once to get a sum.

PROBLEM

21.

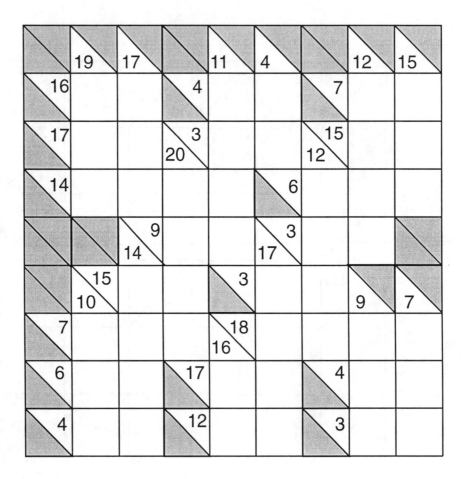

© 1991, 1997 Critical Thinking Books & Software • P.O. Box 448, Pacific Grove, CA 93950 • 800-458-4849

Reference

*Cross-
Number™
Puzzles—
Sums:
Book B-1*

DIRECTIONS

Fill in the grid so that the digits add up to the sums shown.

- A number below a diagonal shows the sum for the squares underneath.

- A number above a diagonal shows the sum for the squares to the right.

- You may use only the digits 1 through 9 (one digit per square).

- You may not use any digit more than once to get a sum.

PROBLEM

22.

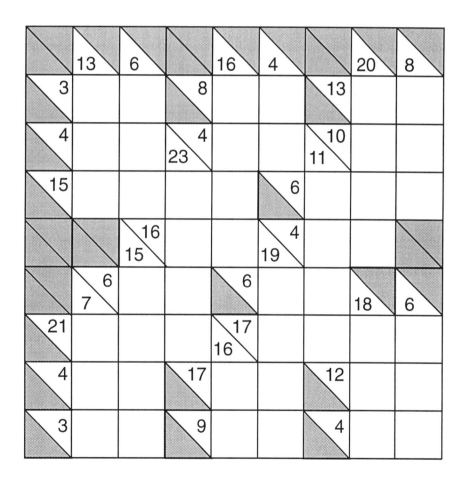

Reference

Critical
Thinking,
Book 1

Inductive
Thinking
Skills

DRAWING INFERENCES

DIRECTIONS

You are given a short story. Tell whether each lettered sentence below the story is true (T), is false (F), or needs more information in order for you to decide (?).

- Accept the story as true. Try to forget anything you heard before about the story. Assume the story uses good English. In general, try to place yourself in the setting of the story.

- Use what you know unless the story says something different. For example, you know what a "house" is, but suppose the story says that only a blue tent can be a "house." Then you must believe the story, and you must not use your own idea of what a "house" is.

PROBLEM

23.   Story

HUMPTY DUMPTY

Humpty Dumpty sat on a wall.

Humpty Dumpty had a great fall.

All the king's horses

And all the king's men

Couldn't put Humpty together again.

a. The wall was high.

b. Humpty fell from the wall.

c. Humpty fell.

Reference

*Critical
Thinking,
Book 1*

*Inductive
Thinking
Skills*

d. Humpty was a female.

e. Humpty was injured.

f. The king's men all tried at the same time to put Humpty together.

g. The king's horses tried to put Humpty together.

h. Humpty was an egg.

i. The king's horses were men.

Reference

Critical
Thinking,
Book 1

Inductive
Thinking
Skills

24. Story

LITTLE JACK HORNER

Little Jack Horner sat in a corner
Eating a Christmas pie.
He put in his thumb and pulled out a plum
And said, "What a good boy am I!"

a. Jack Horner was little.

b. Jack was sitting in a corner while he was eating.

c. Jack was eating a plum pie.

d. Jack was sitting on a chair.

e. Jack was a good boy.

f. Jack thought he was a good boy.

g. The story took place somewhere around Christmas time.

Reference

*Critical
Thinking,
Book 1*

*Inductive
Thinking
Skills*

25. Story

ANTON, MARTHESE, GERDA, AND CUTIE

Anton is five years older than his cousin Marthese, who is three years younger than her cousin Gerda. Gerda has a pet hamster, Cutie.

a. Anton and Gerda are cousins.

b. Marthese and Cutie are cousins.

c. Gerda is older than Marthese.

d. Cutie is younger than Gerda.

e. Cutie is a hamster.

f. If Anton is ten years old, then Gerda is two years old.

Reference

Critical Thinking, Book 1

Inductive Thinking Skills

g. Anton is Gerda's brother.

h. Anton is not related to Gerda.

i. If Marthese is ten years old, then Anton is five years old.

j. If Gerda's age is ten years, then Anton is twelve years old.

k. If Anton is twice as old as Marthese, then Marthese is five years old.

l. Maybe Anton is twice as old as Gerda.

m. If Gerda is thirteen years old, then Marthese's age is two-thirds of Anton's age.

Reference

*Basic
Thinking
Skills*

IDENTIFYING SYNONYMS

DIRECTIONS

Each line contains several words.

Read the first word and think about what it means.

One of the other words will mean almost the same as the first word.

Write this other word.

EXAMPLE

Problem: neat (messy, clean, tidy)
Answer: tidy

PROBLEMS

26. over (delayed, finished, tabled, tentative)

27. seen (detected, sensed, sighted, vista)

28. scene (detected, sensed, sighted, vista)

Reference

*Basic
Thinking
Skills*

29. multiply (raise, enlarge, snowball, extend)

30. censure (cut out, rebuke, receptor, count)

31. censor (cut out, rebuke, receptor, count)

32. sensor (cut out, rebuke, receptor, count)

33. census (cut out, rebuke, receptor, count)

Reference

*Basic
Thinking
Skills*

FINDING COMMON ATTRIBUTES

DIRECTIONS

Each line contains four words.

Read all four words.

They will all have something in common.

Decide what this common thing is, and write it down.

EXAMPLE

Problem: ball, wheel, plate, coin
Answer: round shape

PROBLEMS

34. uncommon, scarce, rare, occasional

35. sum, product, quotient, difference

36. indifferent, neutral, disinterested, unconcerned

37. chief, king, boss, general

38. stir, baste, blend, cream

39. length, width, height, breadth

IDENTIFYING THE OUTSIDER

DIRECTIONS

Read the five given terms.

Four of the terms have something in common.

The other term does not have this same quality.

Tell what the four terms have in common, and tell which term doesn't belong.

EXAMPLE

Problem: nice, big, mean, kind, nasty
Answer: ways to describe personality; big

PROBLEMS

40.   castle, manor, mansion, palace, penthouse

41.   different, experimental, interesting, inventive, new

42.   moan, mumble, murmur, mutter, whisper

43.   bellow, howl, roar, shout, yell

44.   anger, eruption, explosion, outburst, tantrum

45.   alter, change, correct, edit, modify

IDENTIFYING ANALOGOUS RELATIONSHIPS

DIRECTIONS

Each problem takes up two lines. There are two terms on the first line. There are at least four terms on the second line.

On the first line, read the two terms and figure out how they are related. Then go to the second line and find this same relationship between the first term there and one of the other terms there.

Write the word you choose.

EXAMPLE

Problem: kind, unkind

nice, (big, hungry, nasty)

Answer: nasty

PROBLEMS

46.　fast, slow

hare, (greyhound, ostrich, tortoise)

47.　modern, ancient

elephant, (mammoth, griffin, unicorn)

48.　3/4, 9/12

2/3, (8/11, 6/8, 8/12)

49. 2 feet, 1 yard

4 feet, (2 yards, 3 yards, 6 yards, 8 yards)

50. believe, doubt

accept, (pretend, question, reject, deny)

51. accept, reject

prove, (examine, challenge, disagree, contradict)

52. plus, positive

minus, (divide, negative, remainder, subtract)

53. inactive, active

lazy, (conscientious, vigilant, intelligent, lively)

Reference

*Basic
Thinking
Skills*

DIRECTIONS

Each problem takes two or three lines.

There are two terms on the first line. Read these terms and figure out how they are related.

On the other lines are some pairs of terms. Choose the pair whose terms are related in the same way as the terms on the first line.

EXAMPLE

Problem: hard, soft

         (work, play / cement, mud / mud, steel)

Answer: cement, mud

PROBLEMS

54. plus, minus

     (divide, multiply / more, less / negative, positive)

55. male, female

     (gentleman, lady / carpenter, secretary / fire fighter, homemaker)

56. before, after

     (then, there / action, reason / precede, succeed / day, year)

57. dentures, spectacles

(wig, hairpiece / false teeth, eyeglasses / plaster cast, sling)

58. enemy, foe

(neighbor, friend / computer, robot / principal, teacher / friend, ally)

59. sheep, steer

(mutton, beef / lamb, ham / ham, veal / pork, beef)

60. cup, quart

(yard, foot / gram, ounce / quart, gallon / pint, liter)

61. knowledge, fact

(intuition, reason / logic, opinion / deduction, judgment / conjecture, given)

DIRECTIONS

Each problem is given in the form of a chart.

The words for the last two columns are listed (by column, in alphabetical order) below the chart.

Each line of the chart is a small problem by itself.

For each line, read the first two words and decide how they are related. Then find a third and fourth word (from the bottom) that are related in the same way.

EXAMPLE

Problem:

able	unable		
active	inactive		
ask	why		
fleas	dog		
quarter	1/4		

3rd column: alive, answer, can, half, lice

4th column: because, cannot, dead, human, 1/2

Answer:

able	unable	can	cannot
active	inactive	alive	dead
ask	why	answer	because
fleas	dog	lice	human
quarter	1/4	half	1/2

PROBLEMS

62.

+	−		
×	÷		
1/4	1		
−	+		
÷	+		

Column 3: increase, part, product, quotient, take away

Column 4: add to, decrease, quotient, sum, whole

Reference

Basic Thinking Skills

63.

origin	destination		
expand	grow		
help	meddle		
professional	amateur		
quiet	noisy		

Column 3: assist, contract, reserved, start, veteran

Column 4: beginner, end, exuberant, interfere, shrink

STATING ANALOGIES IN STANDARD FORM

LESSON

Suppose we find a relation between two things, and we find the same relation between two other things. Then we say there is an *analogous* (uh NAL uh gus) relationship between the two pairs.

EXAMPLE

There is an analogous relationship between the pair

> hot   cold

and the pair

> steam   ice

To state the analogy (uh NAL uh jee) between the two pairs, we will use the words "is to" and "as":

> *Hot* is to *cold* as *steam* is to *ice*.

DIRECTIONS

Each problem takes two or three lines.

On the first line are a pair of terms. Figure out how they are related.

On the other lines are several pairs of terms. Choose the pair that are analogous to the pair on the first line. Then state the analogy between the two pairs.

EXAMPLE

Problem: hot, cold

> (big, little / ice, steam / steam, ice / right, wrong)

Answer: Hot is to cold as steam is to ice.

PROBLEMS

64. elephant, ant

   (animal, vegetable / strong, weak / large, small / destructive, constructive)

65. elephant, ant

(trees, sand / herd, colony / jungle, plains / warlike, peaceful)

66. linger, hasten

(dawdle, rush / retreat, advance / precede, proceed / lazy, ambitious)

67. repair, maintain

(old, new / fix, ignore / professional, amateur / cure, prevent)

68. acute, obtuse

(thin, thick / needle, nail / sharp, blunt / desperate, unimportant)

69. hammer, saw

(cut, pound / clobber, slice / plumber, carpenter / metal, wood)

REARRANGING ANALOGIES

LESSON

If we find an analogy between two pairs of things, we can rearrange the four things so that there are other analogies, too. For instance, with the two pairs

hot, cold / steam, ice

all of these would be correct:

Hot	is to	cold	as	steam	is to	ice.
Cold	is to	hot	as	ice	is to	steam.
Steam	is to	ice	as	hot	is to	cold.
Ice	is to	steam	as	cold	is to	hot.
Hot	is to	steam	as	cold	is to	ice.
Steam	is to	hot	as	ice	is to	cold.
Cold	is to	ice	as	hot	is to	steam.
Ice	is to	cold	as	steam	is to	hot.

Don't be fooled into thinking an analogy will be correct no matter how you position the terms. There are 24 ways to list 4 terms, and only 8 of these will work. Here are some of the 16 incorrect arrangements for the four terms above:

Hot	is to	cold	as	ice	is to	steam.
Hot	is to	ice	as	cold	is to	steam.
Steam	is to	ice	as	cold	is to	hot.
Cold	is to	ice	as	steam	is to	hot.

> **DIRECTIONS**
>
> You are given four terms. If they can be split into analogous pairs, list at least three correct analogies.

EXAMPLE

Problem: speaker, hear, talk, listener

Answer: (Any three of these would be correct.)

Speaker is to talk as listener is to hear.

Speaker is to listener as talk is to hear.

Hear is to listener as talk is to speaker.

Hear is to talk as listener is to speaker.

Talk is to speaker as hear is to listener.

Talk is to hear as speaker is to listener.

Listener is to speaker as hear is to talk.

Listener is to hear as speaker is to talk.

PROBLEMS

70. bird, nest, lair, lion

71. Canada, China, Asia, North America

72. merchant, buy, sell, customer

73. attorney, dentist, client, patient

74. tennis, bowl, alley, court

DIRECTIONS
This problem is just for fun.
Each one of the four entries is a term for an analogy. The terms are arranged in the right order for an analogy, but they may be disguised by puns, misspellings, homonyms, misleading definitions, and other good things.
Figure out what the correct terms are, and write the analogy.

PROBLEM

75.

metal

football period

male deer

worth of fish structure

© 1991, 1997 Critical Thinking Books & Software • P.O. Box 448, Pacific Grove, CA 93950 • 800-458-4849

PROBLEM

76.

aparsonc

edeedx

nose
the

discarded stage routine

PROBLEM

77.

amusement park ride that's thrilling but with no hair curler

dwow pain

put tahhsittocS

recordless tr

DIRECTIONS

This problem is just for fun.

Each one of the four entries is a term for an analogy. The terms are arranged in the right order for an analogy, but they may be disguised by puns, misspellings, homonyms, misleading definitions, and other good things.

Figure out what the correct terms are, and write the analogy.

PROBLEM

78.

confused blot

timepiece that was sightless at first but not later

bowling target follows vault before beverage

strikes out-of-order an object in fascinating her

PROBLEM

79.

bus coming from the opposite direction leads unique unseeing floor lids

e untied if

able able 10 10 do

1 having a young to-do

(Hint: If the clues seem puzzling because they're too crafty, try putting yourself in my place: I couldn't be too open about them because then they'd be so obvious that you'd have nothing left to figure out.)

Reference

*Inductive
Thinking
Skills*

REASONING BY ANALOGY

LESSON

When you reason by *analogy*, you think, "This situation is a lot like that other situation. Therefore, the same thing will be true now that was true then."

In other words, an analogy looks at two things and says, "They are alike in some ways, so they are also alike in these other ways."

Some analogies are good ones, and some are not.

EXAMPLE 1

When Ezra takes a test, he closes his eyes while he thinks of an answer. He finishes at least 15 minutes early, and he always gets good test grades. I want to get good test grades, so I'm going to close my eyes while I think of an answer, and I'm going to finish at least 15 minutes early.

The two things being compared are (1) what Ezra does when he takes a test and (2) what I will do when I take the same test. I notice two things that Ezra does and that I intend to do, so the situations are alike in at least two ways. I figure that they should also be alike in the test grades Ezra and I get.

This is a very poor analogy. Ezra's test grades depend on the answers he gives, not on whether or not he closes his eyes or finishes early. So the two situations are not enough alike to make my conclusion reasonable.

EXAMPLE 2

Ezra studies before a test and he always gets good test grades. I asked him how he knows what to study, and he told me. I'm as smart as Ezra is, so if I study before a test like Ezra does, I should get good test grades, too.

This is a good analogy. In a case like this, the situations are said to be analogous.

DIRECTIONS

You are told about an analogy someone has used.

Tell whether you think the analogy is pretty good, just okay, poor, or needs more information in order for you to decide.

Whatever you answer, tell why.

PROBLEM

80.   Jaime is in the eighth grade. Up until now, he has not had any trouble learning the material in his mathematics classes.

His regular mathematics class this semester is going pretty much as usual, but he understands very little in his computer programming class, even though he has had extra help from his teacher.

The high school in Jaime's district teaches two computer programming languages, one of which is the language taught in the class Jaime is now taking.

He had planned to enroll in the other class later on, but now he figures that he's just no good at learning to program a computer, and he has decided not to enroll in the other class.

Reference

Inductive Thinking Skills

DIRECTIONS

You are told about an analogy someone has used.

Tell whether you think the analogy is pretty good, just okay, poor, or needs more information in order for you to decide.

Whatever you answer, tell why.

PROBLEM

81. Nigel's mother bakes a batch of the family's favorite cookies about once a month. Nigel found the recipe and tried mixing and baking a batch of the cookies yesterday, and they tasted terrible.

When he went back over the recipe, he realized that he had put in three cups of flour instead of two cups, and he had used baking powder instead of baking soda.

His mother threw the cookies outside for the birds to eat, and Nigel tried again today. The cookies turned out with a different taste than yesterday's, but they're still terrible.

He found that this time he used one and a half cups of cocoa instead of half a cup, and he put in half a tablespoonful of salt instead of half a teaspoonful.

Nigel has decided not to try making those cookies again because something is bound to go wrong if he does.

DIRECTIONS

You are told about an analogy someone has used.

Tell whether you think the analogy is pretty good, just okay, poor, or needs more information in order for you to decide.

Whatever you answer, tell why.

PROBLEM

82. Rosita's aunt Raquel earned a degree in mechanical engineering five years ago and has been very happy in her position with the Wayland Engineering company.

   Rosita, now in the eighth grade, has decided that she will go to college for a degree in mechanical engineering and then work for Wayland Engineering so that she, too, will be happy in her work.

© 1991, 1997 Critical Thinking Books & Software • P.O. Box 448, Pacific Grove, CA 93950 • 800-458-4849

OPERATORS AND ORDER OF PRECEDENCE

LESSON

Addition (+), subtraction (−), multiplication (×), division (÷ or /), and raising to a power (such as 3^2) are arithmetic *operators*.

A problem can include an operator more than once:

$$5 + 3 + 4 = ?$$

It can also include different operators:

$$5 + 3 - 4 = ?$$
$$1 + 2 \times 3 = ?$$

Parentheses can be used to show which operator to start with:

$$(1 + 2) \times 3 = ?$$
$$1 + (2 \times 3) = ?$$

Brackets can be used as a second set of parentheses:

$$15 - [12 - 3 \times (1 + 2)] = ?$$

To solve a problem, we move from left to right, but we must do it in this order:

1.   ( )

2.   [ ]

3.   raise to a power

4.   ×, ÷ or / (These operators are of equal rank. Start at the left, and do whichever one comes first. Keep going, and do whichever one comes next.)

5.   +, − (These operators are of equal rank.)

For the examples below, remember the rules: move from left to right, but first do ( ), then [ ], then raise to a power, then × and ÷ and /, and then + and −.

EXAMPLE 1

Problem: $24 - (5 + 2) \times 3$

Solution: (Steps that are not needed are skipped here.)

Step 1.   Do ( ). So do $5 + 2$. So $24 - (5 + 2) \times 3 = 24 - 7 \times 3$.

Step 4.   Do ×, ÷, and /. There is no ÷ or /, so do 7×3 and get $24 - 7 \times 3 = 24 - 21$.

Step 5.   Do + and −. There is no +, so $24 - 21 = 3$.

Answer: $24 - (5 + 2) \times 3 = 24 - 7 \times 3 = 24 - 21 = 3$

EXAMPLE 2

Problem: $24 - (8 + 2 \times 5) \div 6$

Solution:

Step 1.   Do ( ). So do $8 + 2 \times 5$. This is like example 1 above at the end of step 1. So $8 + 2 \times 5 = 8 + 10 = 18$. The problem is now $24 - 18 \div 6$.

Step 4.   Do ÷. So $24 - 18 \div 6 = 24 - 3$.

Step 5.   Do −. We get $24 - 3 = 21$.

Answer: $24 - (8 + 2 \times 5) \div 6 = 24 - (8 + 10) \div 6 = 24 - 18 \div 6 = 24 - 3 = 21$

EXAMPLE 3

Problem: $5 + 12/(1 + 3) \times 3$

Solution:

Step 1.   Do ( ). We get $5 + 12/(1 + 3) \times 3 = 5 + 12/4 \times 3$.

Step 4.   Do × and /. We go from left to right and get $5 + 12/4 \times 3 = 5 + 3 \times 3 = 5 + 9$.

Step 5.   Do +. We get $5 + 9 = 14$.

Answer: $5 + 12/(1 + 3) \times 3 = 5 + 12/4 \times 3 = 5 + 3 \times 3 = 5 + 9 = 14$

EXAMPLE 4

Problem: $14 - [6 \div 3 + 1 \times (2 + 3)]$

Solution: (Notice that "÷" in the given problem is written as "/" below. The two symbols mean the same thing and can be freely exchanged.)

Step 1.   Do ( ). So do $2 + 3 = 5$. This makes the problem $14 - [6/3 + 1 \times (2 + 3)] = 14 - [6/3 + 1 \times 5]$.

Step 2.   Do [ ]. So do $6/3 + 1 \times 5$. Because $\times$ and $/$ are done before $+$, and because we always work from left to right, we get $6/3 + 1 \times 5 = 2 + 1 \times 5 = 2 + 5 = 7$. Starting from the end of step 1 above, we now have $14 - [6/3 + 1 \times 5] = 14 - 7$.

Step 5.   Do $-$. We get $14 - 7 = 7$.

Answer: $14 - [6 \div 3 + 1 \times (2 + 3)] =$
$14 - [6 \div 3 + 1 \times 5] =$
$14 - [2 + 1 \times 5] = 14 - [2 + 5] = 14 - 7 = 7$

EXAMPLE 5

Problem: $(3 + 12 \div 3) \times (6 - 4 + 2) - 4^2$

Solution:

Step 1.   Do ( ). There are two sets of ( ). We work from left to right, so first we will do $3 + 12 \div 3$, and then we will do $6 - 4 + 2$. We do $\div$ before $+$, so for $3 + 12 \div 3$, we get $3 + 4 = 7$. Taking $6 - 4 + 2$, the $+$ and $-$ have equal rank, so we move left to right and get $6 - 4 + 2 = 2 + 2 = 4$. We now have $(3 + 12 \div 3) \times (6 - 4 + 2) - 4^2 = 7 \times 4 - 4^2$.

Step 3.   Do "raise to a power." So do $4^2 = 16$. The problem is now $7 \times 4 - 4^2 = 7 \times 4 - 16$.

Step 4.   Do $\times$. We get $7 \times 4 - 16 = 28 - 16$.

Step 5.   Do $-$. So $28 - 16 = 12$.

Answer: $(3 + 12 \div 3) \times (6 - 4 + 2) - 4^2 =$
$(3 + 4) \times (6 - 4 + 2) - 4^2 =$
$7 \times (6 - 4 + 2) - 4^2 =$
$7 \times (2 + 2) - 4^2 =$
$7 \times 4 - 4^2 = 7 \times 4 - 16 = 28 - 16 = 12$

EXAMPLE 6

Problem: $20 \div 10/2 \times 7 \times 2^3$

Solution: We don't need steps 1, 2, or 5 for this one. Step 4 says the operators $\times$, $\div$, and / are all of equal rank and we are to work from left to right. We do step 3 and then step 4.

Answer: $20 \div 10/2 \times 7 \times 2^3 =$
$20 \div 10/2 \times 7 \times 8 =$
$2/2 \times 7 \times 8 = 1 \times 7 \times 8 = 7 \times 8 = 56$

Notice how the answer would change if ( ) enclosed 10/2. Then it would be $20 \div (10/2) \times 7 \times 2^3 = 20 \div 5 \times 7 \times 2^3 = 20 \div 5 \times 7 \times 8 = 4 \times 7 \times 8 = 28 \times 8 = 224$.

DIRECTIONS

You are told what answer is wanted. To get this answer, you may use only the numbers 1, 3, and 4, along with two operators. You may *not* use ( ) or [ ]. Show your work in the same way the example below shows the work.

EXAMPLE

Problem: Get an answer of 7.

Answer: $3 + 1 \times 4 = 3 + 4 = 7$

For each answer, you must use each of the numbers 1, 3, and 4 exactly once. You may use the same operator twice if you wish to do so.

There are different ways to get each answer, so do not copy the example's arrangement for your answer.

You are not allowed to combine digits to make a new number. For example, you are not allowed to combine 4 and 3 and get 43. However, raising to a power, such as 4^3, is allowed.

PROBLEMS

83.   Get an answer of 0.

$3 + 1 - 4$

Insert ( ) [ ] if necessary

106. $5 + 13 \div 6 - 4 \times 4$; answer 36

107. $6 + 2 \times 9 - 13 - 7 \times 7$; answer 30

108. $6 \times 9 - 3 \times (7 + 1) - 21$; answer 9

109. $8 \times 10 - 36 \div 9 + 2 - 2 \times 5 \times 5$; answer 0

110. $3^2 + 1 \times 5 - 2 + 4 \times 8$; answer 2

111. $4 \times 10 - 7 - 2 \times 2^3 - 1$; answer 79

112. $3^2 + 2^3 - 24 \div 6 - 4 \times 18 \div 9^2$; answer 20

Insert ( ) [ ] if necessary

Reference

Classroom
Quickies,
Books 1–
3

113. Using the digits 1, 2, 3, and 4, along with any mathematical operators you choose, see how many different numbers you can write.

Here are the rules:

Your answers must be whole numbers.

In each answer, you must use each of the four digits exactly once.

You are allowed to use any mathematical symbols and operators you know about. For example, you may use decimals, and if you know about { } and roots, you may use those, too.

In each answer, you may use any operator as often as you like.

You are allowed to use each digit as a separate number.

You are allowed to combine two or more digits to make a number.

If you combine two digits to make a number, you cannot use an operator to separate the digits. For example, you may use 1 and 2 to make the number 21, but you may not write something like

$$2(4 - 3)$$

to make 21. However, you *are* allowed to use a decimal point between two digits. For example, you could write

$$1.2$$

to make one and two tenths.

EXAMPLES

$$0 = 1 + 4 - 2 - 3$$

$$1 = 2 \times 3 - 4 - 1$$

$$2 = (2 + 4) \div 3 \times 1$$

$$3 = (4 + 2) \times 1 - 3$$

$$4 = 2 \times 4 - 1 - 3$$

$$5 = (4^2 - 1)/3$$

$$6 = 12/4 + 3$$

Reference

Classroom Quickies, Books 1–3

114. This problem is like the preceding one, except that this time you are to use only 4s, along with any mathematical operators you choose. For each problem, you must use at least two 4s, and you may not use more than six 4s. See how many different numbers you can write.

Here are the rules again:

Your answers must be whole numbers.

You are allowed to use any mathematical symbols and operators you know about. For example, you may use decimals, and if you know about { } and roots, you may use them, too.

In each answer, you may use any operator as often as you like.

You are allowed to use each 4 as a separate number.

You are allowed to combine two or more 4s to make a number.

If you combine two or more 4s to make a number, you cannot use an operator to separate the digits. For example, you may use two 4s to make the number 44, but you may not write something like

$$4(4 + 4 - 4)$$

to make 44. However, you *are* allowed to use a decimal point between two digits. For example, you could write

$$4.4$$

to make four and four tenths.

EXAMPLES

$$0 = 4 - 4$$

$$1 = 4 \div 4$$

$$2 = (4 + 4)/4$$

$$3 = 4 - 4/4$$

$$4 = 4 \times 4/4$$

$$5 = 4 + 4/4$$

$$6 = 4 + (4 + 4)/4$$

Reference

Basic Thinking Skills

FOLLOWING DIRECTIONS

DIRECTIONS

Take a sheet of paper and a pencil (or pen).

Each part of the problem tells you to do something.

Do it all on the same sheet of paper.

PROBLEM

115. a. Draw a diamond in about the center of your paper.

b. Draw a segment from the top vertex of the diamond to the upper-right corner of your paper.

c. Going clockwise from part b, both for the vertices of the diamond and for the corners of your paper, draw three other segments.

d. Write your name on the third segment drawn.

e. If today is Monday or Tuesday or if tomorrow or the day after will be Friday or Sunday or if yesterday was Saturday, then draw a five-pointed star at the right edge of your paper about halfway down. Otherwise, draw a circle at the left edge of your paper, about halfway up.

f. Find all of the prime factors of 462. Write these in numerical order just below the top edge of your paper starting from the left.

g. Multiply 5 by each answer from part f. Write each product below the corresponding multiplier.

h. Add the answers from part g. Write the sum inside the diamond.

i. Add the answers from part f. Multiply the sum by 5. Write the product below the answer to part h.

Reference

*Basic
Thinking
Skills*

DRAWING INFERENCES

DIRECTIONS

Sometimes a problem needs only a "yes" or "no" answer, but be ready to tell why you chose your answer if you are asked about it.

Sometimes a problem doesn't tell you enough to let you know for sure what the answer is. In this case, answer "not enough information."

PROBLEMS

116. Read the three sentences below and then answer the question that follows.

   a. Everyone in Irwin's class took a test today.
   b. Irwin did not fail the test.
   c. Irwin did not pass the test.

   Can all three of these sentences be true? Explain.

117. Limetown is 10 kilometers from Big City and 15 kilometers from Appleton.

   Appleton is 5 kilometers from Big City.

   Can all three cities lie in a straight line? Explain.

118. Oakton is 20 kilometers from Big City and 15 kilometers from Elmtown.

   Elmtown is 10 kilometers from Big City.

   Can all three cities lie in a straight line? Explain.

MISCELLANEOUS PROBLEMS

PROBLEMS

119. If Joanna starts counting at 65 and keeps counting until she finishes at 5135, how many numbers has she counted?

Assume she counts accurately. (She counts 65, 66, ..., 5134, 5135.)

120. An automatic turntable holding six long-playing records (LP's) is started.

The first LP drops and starts playing.

Each LP lasts for twenty minutes, and it takes twenty seconds after one LP finishes before the next LP starts.

How long will it be until the sixth LP stops playing?

Reference

Basic
Thinking
Skills

Math
Word
Problems

121. What's the difference between two dozen half-dozens and a dozen dozens?

122. What's the difference between half a dozen half-dozens and half of a half-dozen?

123. What's the difference between a half-dozen dozen, half a dozen dozen, and a dozen half-dozens?

A "baker's dozen" is 13 because bakers used to count out 13, not 12, items when someone ordered a dozen of the item. Why did bakers do this? How many items did someone get if the order was for half a dozen? How come when you go to a bakery today and order a dozen doughnuts, you get only 12?

Reference

Classroom Quickies, Books 1–3

REARRANGE LETTERS

DIRECTIONS

Use the letters at the top to fill in the chart so that words are formed and the sentence makes sense.

- A shaded space in the chart shows the end of a word.

- Except for the last line, the end of a line is not the end of a word unless there is a shaded space there.

- When you have filled in the chart, answer the question asked.

PROBLEM

124.

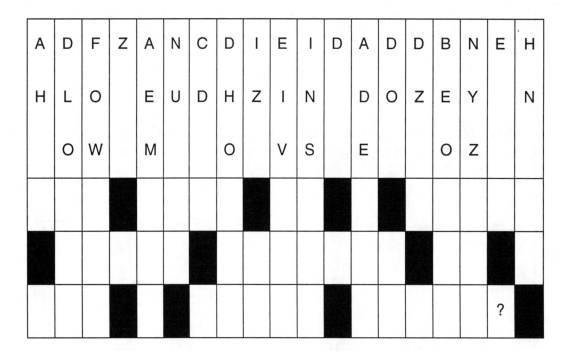

References

*Algebra
Word
Problems—
Diophantine
Problems*

*Classroom
Quickies,
Books 1–
3*

DIOPHANTINE PROBLEMS

PROBLEM

125. Angelica and her brother, Morton, had a total of $100 they earned washing walls.

They heard about a fantastic garage sale and went to see what they could find.

When they saw the prices for paperback books, jeans, and winter jackets, they decided to buy 100 items with their $100.

If the jackets were $9 each, the jeans $3 a pair, and the books 5 for $1, how many of each did they buy?

There are about $365\frac{1}{4}$ days in a year. That's why we have leap years— one extra day every four years.

Reference

Classroom Quickies, Book 1–3

WATER JUGS PROBLEMS

PROBLEM

126. You have three jugs and a river of clean water.

The jugs are known to hold exactly 3, 5, and 9 quarts.

Tell how you can use these jugs to measure exactly 6 quarts of water.

Why did the 15 year old who had just moved into the neighborhood take a ladder with him the first time he went to his new school?

CLOCK ARITHMETIC

LESSON

Suppose we had a clock that went only from 1 to 8 instead of from 1 to 12. We could do the same kind of arithmetic with it that we do for a 12-hour clock.

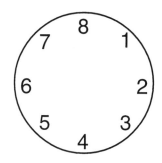

With a 12-hour clock, we count from 1 to 12 and then start over. With an 8-hour clock, we would count from 1 to 8 and then start over.

EXAMPLES

If it is 5 o'clock now, then 4 hours from now it will be 1 o'clock.

If it is 2 o'clock now, then 2 hours ago it was 8 o'clock, and 3 hours ago it was 7 o'clock.

DIRECTIONS

You are told what time it is now. You are asked to find a different time. Use an 8-hour clock.

EXAMPLE

Problem: 7 o'clock; 2 hours from now
Answer: 1 o'clock

PROBLEMS

127. 7 o'clock; 3 hours from now

128. 3 o'clock; 3 hours ago

129. 6 o'clock; 8 hours from now

130. 6 o'clock; 8 hours ago

131. 5 o'clock; 6 hours from now

132. 4 o'clock; 9 hours from now

133. 2 o'clock; 11 hours ago

134. 7 o'clock; 10 hours ago

DIRECTIONS

Now try analogous ideas on other clocks.

EXAMPLE

Problem: 6-hour clock; now 5 o'clock; 3 hours from now
Answer: 2 o'clock

PROBLEMS

135. 6-hour clock; now 5 o'clock; 7 hours from now

136. 7-hour clock; now 2 o'clock; 5 hours ago

137. 10-hour clock; now 8 o'clock; 7 hours from now

138. 4-hour clock; now 3 o'clock; 3 hours from now

139. 9-hour clock; now 4 o'clock; 15 hours from now

140. 9-hour clock; now 2 o'clock; 24 hours ago

141. 3-hour clock; now 1 o'clock; 14 hours from now

142. 3-hour clock; now 1 o'clock; 14 hours ago

143. 10-hour clock; now 9 o'clock; 12 hours ago

144. 7-hour clock; now 5'clock; 10 hours ago

145. MARIO'S METHOD FOR CLOCK ARITHMETIC

Mario says he has a fast way of doing clock arithmetic. He gave these examples:

"Suppose it's a 6-hour clock. If my answer is more than 6, I subtract 6. If it's going to be less than 1, I add 6. Say it's 4 o'clock and I want 5 hours from now. I take 4 + 5 and get 9. That's more than 6, so I subtract 6 and get 3, and the answer is 3 o'clock.

"Or say it's 1 o'clock and I want 3 hours ago. If I take 1 − 3, I'll get less than 1, so I add 6 first. I take 1 + 6 − 3 and get 4, so the answer is 4 o'clock."

Julia asked what happens if his answer is still more than 6 for a 6-hour clock. He said he keeps subtracting 6s until the answer is between 1 and 6. Julia used Mario's method to find the time 8 hours after 5 o'clock. She took 8 + 5 − 6 − 6 and got 1 o'clock, and that answer is correct.

Loretta asked Mario what he does for a 6-hour clock if the problem says to find the time 16 hours ago if it's 2 o'clock now. He said he keeps adding 6s to the 2 until he gets a number more than 16, and then he subtracts.

a. Do you think Mario's method will *always* work for a 6-hour clock? If so, how come? If not, give a counterexample.

b. 1) What would Mario's method be for a 9-hour clock?

   2) Do you think his method will work for a 9-hour clock? If so, how come? If not, give a counterexample.

c. Do you think Mario's method will work for other clocks? If so, how come? If not, give a counterexample.

146. CHOON-WEI'S METHOD FOR CLOCK ARITHMETIC

Choon-Wei said she has a fast method for doing clock arithmetic, too.

For a 6-hour clock, she does the same as Mario if the hours to be added or subtracted are less than 6. But if those hours are more than 6, she subtracts 6s right away.

Choon-Wei gave these examples:

> "Say it's 3 o'clock now and I want to know the time 14 hours from now. I take 14 – 6 – 6 and get 2, and then I add that to 3 and get 5, so it will be 5 o'clock then.

> "Or say it's 3 o'clock now and I want the time 14 hours ago. I take 14 – 6 – 6 and get 2, and I subtract that from 3 and get 1, so it was 1 o'clock then."

Larry said her method wouldn't work for a problem like 14 hours ago if it's 1 o'clock now because 14 – 6 – 6 is 2, and 1 – 2 is less than 1. Choon-Wei said he was wrong because his example reduced the problem to finding the time 2 hours ago if it's 1 o'clock now, and she already said that she uses Mario's method for that kind of problem.

a. Do you think Choon-Wei's method will *always* work for a 6-hour clock? If so, how come? If not, give a counterexample.

b. Suppose Choon-Wei uses analogous reasoning for a 7-hour clock. How would she find the time 15 hours from now if it is now 2 o'clock?

c. Do you think Choon-Wei's method will work for other clocks? If so, how come? If not, give a counterexample.

LESSON CONT.

We have used clock arithmetic on different clocks and found that the arithmetic is analogous for all clocks.

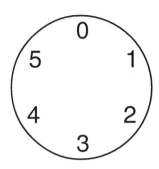

Now think about a 6-hour clock whose 6 has been replaced with 0. The clock will still have 6 numbers, but they will go from 0 through 5 instead of from 1 through 6.

Suppose it is now 1 o'clock. Then 5 hours from now it should be 6 o'clock. But our clock has 0 instead of 6, so it will be 0 o'clock.

We will work problems the same way we would work them if the clock's numbers were 1 through 6. There will be no change unless we get a final answer of 6, in which case our answer will be 0 instead.

EXAMPLES

Problem: Find the time 3 hours after 5 o'clock.

Solution: $5 + 3 = 8$. The clock numbers don't go that far, so we subtract 6 and get $8 - 6 = 2$.

Answer: 2 o'clock

Problem: Find the time 14 hours after 4 o'clock.

Solution: $4 + 14 = 18$. That's too much, so subtract 6. $18 - 6 = 12$. That's still too much, so subtract another 6. $12 - 6 = 6$. Our clock doesn't go up to 6, so we subtract another 6. $6 - 6 = 0$.

Answer: 0 o'clock

Problem: Find the time 7 hours before 3 o'clock.

Solution: $3 - 7$ is less than 0, so we will add 6. We will get $6 + 3 - 7 = 9 - 7 = 2$.

Answer: 2 o'clock

DIRECTIONS

You have a 6-hour clock whose numbers run from 0 through 5. You are asked to find the time some number of hours before or after a given starting time.

EXAMPLE

Problem: Now 4 o'clock; 7 hours later

Solution: $4 + 7 = 11$; $11 - 6 = 5$

Answer: 5 o'clock.

PROBLEMS

147. Now 1 o'clock; 7 hours later

148. Now 3 o'clock; 5 hours earlier

149. Now 5 o'clock; 13 hours later

150. Now 0 o'clock; 11 hours later

151. Now 2 o'clock; 10 hours earlier

152. Now 4 o'clock; 20 hours from now

153. Now 4 o'clock; 20 hours ago

LESSON CONT.

In the United States, the official time period known as a day starts at 12 midnight, written as either

12 midnight   or   12 A.M.

The A.M. hours continue from 12 midnight until 12 noon, which is written as

12 noon   or   12 P.M.

The P.M. hours last from 12 noon until 12 midnight.

To do clock arithmetic for a real-life 12-hour clock, we need to know whether the answer is A.M. or P.M.

This is easy to do if we use a 24-hour clock for our figuring. On a 24-hour clock, the A.M. hours start at 24 and go through 11. The P.M. hours start at 12 and go through 23.

When given a problem, we will first convert the starting time to the time on a 24-hour clock. Then we will do the problem. After we have decided whether the hour is A.M. or P.M., we will convert the answer to 12-hour clock time.

EXAMPLE 1

Problem: It is 3 A.M. now. What time will it be 10 hours from now?

Solution: 3 A.M. = 3 on a 24-hour clock. 3 + 10 = 13, which is a P.M. hour. 13 on this clock is 1 on a 12-hour clock, so it will be 1 P.M.

EXAMPLE 2

Problem: It is 3 A.M. now. What time was it 10 hours ago?

Solution: 3 A.M. = 3 on a 24-hour clock. 3 − 10 is negative, so add 24 to 3. Then 27 − 10 = 17, which is a P.M. hour. 17 − 12 = 5 on a 12-hour clock, so the answer is 5 P.M.

DIRECTIONS

You are given the time now on a 12-hour clock and are asked to find the time some hours before or after that.

Include A.M. or P.M. in your answer.

PROBLEMS

154. Now 2 P.M.; 5 hours from now

155. Now 2 P.M.; 4 hours ago

156. Now 4 A.M.; 9 hours from now

157. Now 4 A.M.; 9 hours ago

158. Now 6 P.M.; 8 hours from now

159. Now 10 A.M.; 6 hours from now

160. Now 5 P.M.; 8 hours ago

161. Now 7 P.M.; 65 hours from now

162. Now 6 A.M.; 65 hours ago

163. Given that we'll use a 24-hour clock so that we'll know whether our answer is A.M. or P.M., why bother to convert the starting time to 24-hour clock time?

That is, why not leave the starting time alone and just add to it or subtract from it the hours in the problem, and then convert the answer if it needs converting?

For example, if it's 3 P.M. now, then 7 hours from now it will be 3 + 7 = 10 P.M. We don't have to bother converting 3 to 15, getting 15 + 7 = 22, and then converting 22 to 10.

LESSON CONT.

The U.S. Armed Forces and many scientific laboratories use a 24-hour clock.

This clock is numbered from 100 through 2400 instead of from 1 through 24. In other words, each hour is shown as 100 times that hour.

At 6 P.M. the time is said to be 1800. On this clock, the time 3 hours after 1800 is 2100.

DIRECTIONS

You are given the time on a clock used by the U.S. military forces.

You are asked to find the time some hours before or after the given time.

Keep in mind that the clock numbers are 100 times the actual numbers, so you will either have to divide a clock number by 100 or multiply the number of hours by 100 before you can compute with them.

EXAMPLE

Problem: Now 0300; 7 hours ago

Solution 1: Convert 7 hours to 700 clock hours. 300 – 700 is less than 100, so add 2400 to 300. Then the time asked for is 2700 – 700 = 2000.

Solution 2: Convert 0300 to 3. 3 – 7 is less than 1, so add 24 to 3. Then 27 – 7 = 20. Convert 20 to clock hours, 2000, to get the time asked for.

PROBLEMS

164. Now 0300; 14 hours from now

---

165.   Now 0300; 14 hours ago

166.   Now 1600; 20 hours from now

167.   Now 2100; 8 hours from now

168.   Now 600; 10 hours ago

169.   Now 2400; 24 hours ago

170.   Now 1850; 7 hours from now

REARRANGE LETTERS

DIRECTIONS

Use the letters at the top to fill in the chart so that words are formed and the sentence makes sense.

- A shaded space in the chart shows the end of a word.

- Except for the last line, the end of a line is not the end of a word unless there is a shaded space there.

- When you have filled in the chart, answer the question asked.

PROBLEM

171.

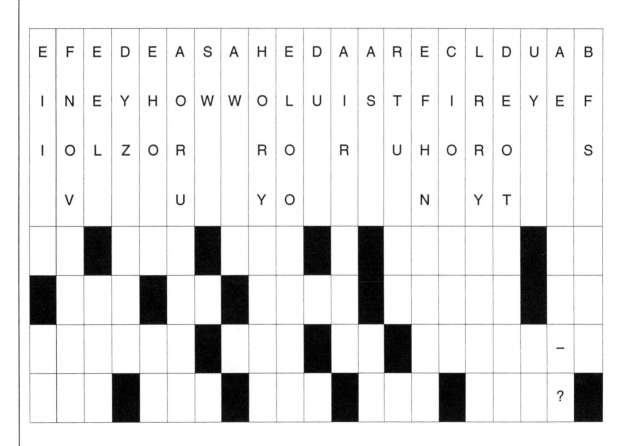

References

Classroom Quickies, Books 1–3

WATER JUGS PROBLEMS

PROBLEM

172. You have three jugs and a well from which to draw water.

The jugs are known to hold exactly 2, 4, and 7 gallons.

Tell how you can use these jugs to measure exactly 12 gallons of water.

DRAWING INFERENCES

PROBLEM

173. The Freeman family uses more water than the Trainor family uses.

Both families buy water from the same water company.

Neither family uses someone else's water supply.

Tell whether or not the Freeman family has a higher water bill than the Trainor family, and tell why.

Reference

*Classroom
Quickies,
Book 3*

MISCELLANEOUS PROBLEMS

PROBLEMS

174. If you buy a bicycle for $20 and sell it for $30 and then buy it back again for $40 and then sell it again for $50, how much money did you gain or lose all together on these deals?

Reference

*Math
Word
Problems*

175. A 9 ft × 12 ft room has a bare floor except for a square mat, 4 ft per side, in its center.

a. What is the area of the part of the floor not covered by the mat?

b. Suppose we move the mat so that it is 1 ft from each of two adjacent walls.

Then what is the area of the part of the floor not covered by the mat?

c. Suppose we move the mat so that one corner of it is in a corner of the floor. (Two sides of the mat will then run 4 ft. along each of the two sides of the room.)

Then what is the area of the part of the floor not covered by the mat?

d. Suppose we move the mat back to the center of the floor, but we cut out a square, 2 ft per side, in the middle of the mat.

Now what is the area of the part of the floor not covered by the mat?

Reference

Math
Word
Problems

176. An adult human is 65% oxygen, 18% carbon, 10% hydrogen, 3% nitrogen, 1.5% calcium, 1% phosphorus, and 1.5% other elements.

Suppose all of these elements weighed the same. For example, given a total body weight of 100 pounds, suppose that the 65% oxygen weighed 65 pounds and 10% hydrogen weighed 10 pounds.

Then if an adult weighed 180 pounds, how much of that weight would be

a. oxygen?

b. carbon?

c. hydrogen?

d. nitrogen?

e. calcium?

f. phosphorus?

g. other elements?

OTHER BASES

LESSON, PART I

Think about the way we write numbers. We start with only ten digits:

0 1 2 3 4 5 6 7 8 9

The first digit, 0, is for zero. After that, they mean 0 + 1, 0 + 2, 0 + 3, and so on up through 0 + 9.

We don't invent new digits when we want to write a number past 9. Instead, we use what we already have, but we write them side by side:

10 11 12 13 14 15 16 17 18 19

Notice that this row of numbers is exactly like the top row except that each number in this row starts with 1. This 1 means that we've used all ten of our digits once before, and we've started over again.

The first symbol here, 10, is for ten because we had ten digits. After that, they mean 10 + 1, 10 + 2, 10 + 3 and so on up through 10 + 9.

After we've written 19, we've used our ten digits twice apiece, so each number in the next row starts with 2:

20 21 22 23 24 25 26 27 28 29

The first symbol here, 20, is for two tens, 2×10. After that, they mean $(2 \times 10) + 1$, $(2 \times 10) + 2$, $(2 \times 10) + 3$ and so on up through $(2 \times 10) + 9$.

We keep going the same way up through the 90s:

90 91 92 93 94 95 96 97 98 99

This time the first symbol, 90, is for nine tens, 9×10. The others mean $(9 \times 10) + 1$, $(9 \times 10) + 2$, $(9 \times 10) + 3$ and so on up through $(9 \times 10) + 9$.

When we reached 90, we had used all ten of our digits 9 times before. Now that we've written 99, we've used all ten digits 10 times, and we have no digits left to write a higher number.

We had an analogous problem after we wrote the number 9. We had used all ten digits once and had to think of a way to write ten, the next number after nine.

We solved that problem by starting at 0 again but writing 1 to the left of 0 to show that the ten digits had all been used one time before.

We will solve this problem in an analogous way. We'll start at 0 again but write 10 to the left of it to show that we've used all ten digits ten times: $100 = 10 \times 10$.

To be more exact, 100 really means

$$1 \times (10 \times 10) \quad + \quad 0 \times 10 \quad + \quad 0 \times 1.$$

Here are some other examples:

$$205 = 2 \times (10 \times 10) \quad + \quad 0 \times 10 \quad + \quad 5 \times 1$$

$$359 = 3 \times (10 \times 10) \quad + \quad 5 \times 10 \quad + \quad 9 \times 1$$

Notice that we write numbers in a special way:

The last digit (on the right) tells how many 1s there are.

$$7 = 7 \times 1$$

The digit to the left of it tells how many 10s there are.

$$37 = 3 \times 10 \quad + \quad 7 \times 1$$

The digit to the left of that one tells how many (10×10)s there are.

$$637 = 6 \times (10 \times 10) \quad + \quad 3 \times 10 \quad + \quad 7 \times 1$$

LESSON, PART II

Because we use ten different digits to write numbers, we say that we use a *base* of ten to write them, or that we write them in *base ten*.

Look at 637 again. Each place held by a digit means something different. Going from right to left, the first digit is in the 1s place, the second digit is in the 10s place, and the third digit is in the (10×10)'s place.

For a four-digit number, the fourth digit would be in the $(10 \times 10 \times 10)$'s place and so on.

Now suppose we didn't have ten different digits. Suppose there were only five different digits—0, 1, 2, 3, and 4. Then we would write the numbers in base five.

34 in base five = (in either base five or base ten) $3 \times 5 + 4 =$ (in base ten) $15 + 4 = 19$.

Notice that we don't write "34 = 19" because that wouldn't make sense. Neither can we write "base 5" (because there is no 5 in base five) or "base 10" (because 10 means different things in different bases).

We could show the bases by subscripts:

$$34_{five} = (3 \times 5 + 4)_{ten} = (15 + 4)_{ten} = 19_{ten}.$$

Or we could use columns:

Base five	Base ten
34	$3 \times 5 + 4 = 15 + 4 = 19$
201	$2 \times (5 \times 5) + 0 \times 5 + 1 \times 1 = 50 + 0 + 1 = 51$
37	Cannot convert. There is no 7 in base five.

177. Write the numbers from one through sixteen in base five.

178. Write the numbers from one through nineteen in base six.

179. Write the numbers from one through twenty-two in base seven.

180. Write the numbers from one through twenty-five in base eight.

181. In the problems above, the last base ten numbers were 16, 19, 22, 25. For the first three of these, notice the difference between each number and the next one.

You should see that this difference has something to do with the last number you wrote for each of the four problems.

a. Suppose you were to write two lists of numbers, one in base ninety-six* and the other in base ninety-seven, starting at 1 and ending at $81_{\text{ninety-six}}$ and $81_{\text{ninety-seven}}$. In base ten, these last numbers would not be the same.

Without converting $81_{\text{ninety-six}}$ and $81_{\text{ninety-seven}}$ to base ten, tell what would be the difference in base ten between these two numbers, and tell how you know.

b. Same question as for part a, except the last numbers were $85_{\text{ninety-six}}$ and $85_{\text{ninety-seven}}$.

---

* We'd have to use different symbols to count past 9. For bases through base thirty-six, capital block letters are used. Please see the following example:

base ten: 1 2 3 4 5 6 7 8 9 10 11 12 13 14 15

base twelve: 1 2 3 4 5 6 7 8 9 A B 10 11 12 13

182. Think about how you add numbers in base ten. For example, to do this problem

$$247$$
$$+ 56$$

you start by adding 7 and 6. You get 13, which can't all go in the 1s column, so you enter 3 in the 1s column and carry the other 10 to the 10s column.

$$1$$
$$247$$
$$+ 56$$
$$3$$

That's 1 ten you've carried there, so that column now has (1 + 4 + 5) tens = 10 tens. You can't put 10 in one column, so you enter 0 there and carry the other 10 to the next column.

$$11$$
$$247$$
$$+ 56$$
$$03$$

That's 1 ten × ten you've carried there, so that column now has (1 + 2) ten × tens = 3 ten × tens.

$$11$$
$$247$$
$$+ 56$$
$$303$$

All right, so now that we've examined that, see if you can use analogous reasoning to figure out how to add in base eight. While you're at it, see if you can figure out how to subtract in base eight, too. Here's how to go about it:

Make up some base eight addition problems. When you get an answer to each problem, convert the problem and the answer to base ten. Check the addition in base ten to make sure that your base eight answer is right.

When you're sure that your base eight addition is right, try some base eight subtraction. Check your work by converting the base eight numbers to base ten and then subtracting in base ten.

LESSON CONT.

Going from right to left, the place values of a base five number are (in base ten):   1   5   25 (= 5 × 5)   125 (= 5 × 5 × 5)   625 (= 5 × 5 × 5 × 5) and so on.

You know how to convert numbers from base five to base ten. Now suppose you have a base ten number that you want to write in base five. Here are the steps:

Step 1.   Ask, What is the highest place value of five that goes into the base ten number?

Step 2.   Ask, How many whole times will that value go into the number?

Step 3.   The answer to (2) will be the first digit of the base five number.

Step 4.   Multiply (1) by (2) and subtract the answer from the base ten number.

Step 5.   Repeat steps (1) through (4) until your base ten number is less than 5. This final number is the last digit of your base five number.

EXAMPLE

Problem: Convert 366_{ten} to base five.

Solution: 1) 625 is too large, so the highest place value is 125.

2) 125 goes into 366 twice.

3) The first digit of the base five number is 2.

4) 2 × 125 = 250; 366 – 250 = 116.

Return to step 1:

1) 25 is the highest place value of five that will go into 116.

2) 25 goes into 116 four times.

3) The second digit of the base five number is 4. The base five number is 24 so far.

4) 4 × 25 = 100; 116 – 100 = 16.

Return to step 1 again:

1) The highest place value is now 5.

2) 5 goes into 16 three times.

3) The next digit of the base five number is 3, so the base five number is 243 so far.

4) 3 × 5 = 15; 16 – 15 = 1.

5) 1 is the last digit, so the base five number is 2431.

Answer: $366_{ten} = 2431_{five}$

DIRECTIONS

Each number is written in base ten. Convert it to a base five number.

PROBLEMS

183. 65

184. 119

185. 326

186. 1414

187. 3500

DIRECTIONS

Each number is written in base ten. Convert it to the base indicated.
Use reasoning analogous to the reasoning used for converting base ten
numbers to base five numbers.

PROBLEMS

188. 45; six

189. 79; eight

190. 92; seven

191. 539; nine

192. 86; four

Convert each number to a base ten number and then to the base indicated.

EXAMPLE

Problem: 123_{five}; eight

Solution: 123_{five} = (in base ten) $1 \times (5 \times 5) + 2 \times 5 + 3 \times 1 = 25 + 10 + 3 = 38 = 4 \times 8 + 6 = 46_{eight}$

Answer: $123_{five} = 38_{ten} = 46_{eight}$

PROBLEMS

193. 23_{four}; five

194. 221_{three}; six

195. 244_{five}; eight

196. 317_{eight}; five

197. 127_{nine}; seven

198. 345_{six}; nine

199. 3123_{four}; six

200. 1001010_{two}; four

References

Classroom Quickies, Books 1–3

REARRANGE LETTERS

DIRECTIONS

Use the letters at the top to fill in the chart so that words are formed and the sentence makes sense.

- A shaded space in the chart shows the end of a word.

- Except for the last line, the end of a line is not the end of a word unless there is a shaded space there.

- When you have filled in the chart, answer the question asked.

PROBLEM

201.

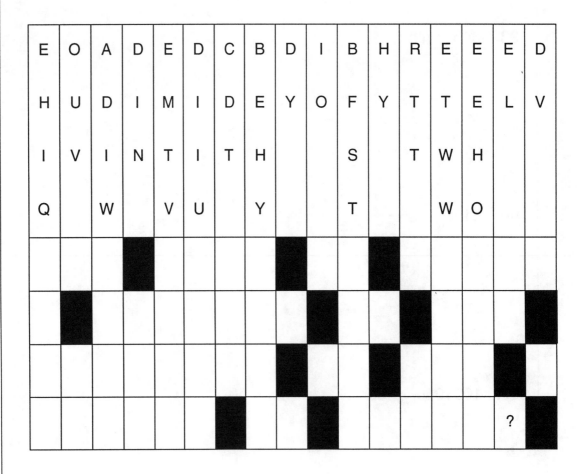

Miscellaneous Problems

Problem

202. A rocket ship was launched at 7:00 A.M. last Tuesday.

The first two rocket stages separated satisfactorily, but when the third stage separated from the command module, it took with it the landing module needed for exploring Mars.

In order to recover the landing module, the command module was manipulated to dock with the third stage.

A few minutes after docking, the command module and the third stage were traveling at a speed of 21,280 feet per second.

Exactly how many miles per hour was this? (Write the answer as a mixed number.)

(Hint: If you use a calculator, you should get something after the decimal point. This is a never-ending decimal fraction, and you'll have to figure out how to express it as a common fraction.)

References

Classroom Quickies, Books 1– 3

WEIGHING BALLS

PROBLEM

203. You have six balls, all of which look exactly the same.

Five of them all weigh the same, but the sixth one is known to be slightly lighter.

You have a balance scale. How can you find the odd ball in at most two weighings?

Reference

*Inductive
Thinking
Skills*

RELEVANT INFORMATION

LESSON

Suppose you are thinking about whether or not to get your hair cut.

You tell your friend James, and he makes a comment.

If his comment is supposed to help you reach a decision, then his comment is *relevant* (REL uh vuhnt). Otherwise, his comment is irrelevant, or not relevant.

EXAMPLE

Problem: Should you get your hair cut or not?

Relevant comments from James:

You look better with your hair as it is now.

Will you have enough money to pay for it?

Your hair is too long now.

Your hair isn't long enough now.

Irrelevant comments, or comments that are not relevant:

My brother got his hair cut yesterday.

You have brown eyes.

My mother always cuts my hair.

You got your hair cut two weeks ago, didn't you?

We say that a statement (or question) is relevant to a subject if that statement (or question) has a bearing upon the subject.

A relevant statement (or question) always has a logical connection with the subject.

DIRECTIONS

A problem is stated and is followed by several lettered sentences.

For each lettered sentence, tell whether or not it is relevant to the problem.

PROBLEMS

204. Louis pulls a lot of practical jokes.

Some of them are really funny, like the time he put on makeup and a girl's wig between two of his classes and told his next teacher that Louis was ill and so she, Louis's sister, was going to sit in the class and then tell Louis what was taught that day.

But some of the jokes could harm other people, like the time he pulled the chair out from under Emilio. Emilio wasn't hurt, but he could've cracked his tailbone if he hadn't landed right.

A couple of Louis's friends tried to talk to him about it, but he just laughed it off. Some of his friends are discussing the problem now of how to make Louis realize that some of his practical jokes are downright dangerous.

a. He should be able to realize it himself, without anyone having to point it out to him.

b. Let's go get a pizza, and we can eat while we're talking about this.

c. We could ask his school counselor to talk to him about it.

Reference

*Inductive
Thinking
Skills*

d. He'd be more likely to pay attention if we all went to see him at the same time.

e. We should make a list of the harmful things that could have happened when he pulled some of his practical jokes.

f. The trouble is, he just assumes that the joke will come off the way he thinks of it, and he doesn't stop to realize what could happen if something goes wrong.

g. Let's think of several practical jokes to pull on Louis. Then every time he pulls one on someone, we'll pull one on him as soon as we can. When he's the butt of a series of jokes, he'll realize that it's no fun to be laughed at, and maybe he'll lay off.

h. It's going to be hard to convince Louis because he always looks on the bright side of things.

Reference

*Inductive
Thinking
Skills*

205. Betty, who is fourteen years old, gets a small weekly allowance from her parents, who can't really afford to make her allowance any higher.

She is making a list of ways to earn money so that she will be able to buy birthday and Christmas presents for her family.

She also wants to have money of her own for various other things that come up, such as attending a school play or buying a paperback book or treating herself to a new headscarf.

Here are some of the comments her friends made when she asked for suggestions for her list.

a. Are you old enough to get a paper route?

b. How about baby-sitting?

c. How can you stand the idea of going out to work? I wouldn't even *think* of it for myself!

d. Are you sure your parents can't increase your allowance?

e. It's too bad you're not a boy because there are more jobs for boys than for girls.

Reference

*Inductive
Thinking
Skills*

f. If you can sew, you can use scraps of material to make things like rag dolls and pot holders and then sell them door-to-door.

g. I can show you how to make gorgeous greeting cards from flower petals and onionskin paper.

h. You may not be able to earn enough to buy everything you'd like to buy.

i. Maybe some of your neighbors would pay you to do jobs they don't like to do, like cleaning a garage or a basement.

j. I don't think there's enough time between now and Christmas to earn enough to buy presents for everyone.

Reference

Inductive Thinking Skills

206. Edith's teacher has finished explaining today's lesson. She says, "Now I'll tell you what your homework is." Edith is ready to make notes about the assignment.

Tell which of the teacher's statements and questions are relevant to these notes.

a. Now where did I put my lesson plans book?

b. I assigned all of the problems on page 87 to last year's class.

c. Do the odd problems on page 74.

d. You did the problems on page 129 for today, right?

e. Find problem 5 in the assignment. Change "are" to "have been."

Reference

*Inductive
Thinking
Skills*

f. We have about 15 minutes of the class period left, so you can start on the homework now.

g. Who has questions about today's lesson?

h. Take a fast look through the problems, and see if you have questions about them.

i. In problem 9, see where it says "look through"— it means "look at."

j. Instead of doing the problems in order, you might find it easier to do number 3 first, then number 7, and then go back to number 1.

NUMBER PATTERNS

DIRECTIONS

Copy each problem.

Each problem lists some numbers and some blanks.

Find a pattern formed by the numbers listed.

Fill in the blanks so that the pattern is continued.

(You may find more than one pattern. If so, use any pattern you find.)

EXAMPLE

Problem: 1, 2, 3, 4, __, __, __, __

One answer: 1, 2, 3, 4, _5_, _6_, _7_, _8_ (Here, the pattern is a simple counting pattern.)

Another answer: 1, 2, 3, 4, _7_, _8_, _15_, _16_ (Here is the pattern: Add the first two numbers to get the next number, add 1 to get the number after that, add the two new numbers to get the third new number, add 1 to get the next number, and continue in the same way.)

PROBLEMS

207. 1, 3, 7, 9, 13, __, __, __, __

208. 1, 4, 2, 8, 6, 24, __, __, __, __

209. 1, 2, 3, 6, 7, 14, __, __, __, __

210. 1, 4, 2, 6, 3, 8, 4, __, __, __, __

211. 5, 6, 8, 11, 15, __, __, __, __

DIRECTIONS

For each problem, at least three parts are shown. The next part has a question mark.

Figure out what was done to the first part to get the second part.

See if the same thing was done to the second part to get the third part. (If it wasn't, go back and start again.)

There is a pattern followed to get each change. Find the pattern and then use it to replace the question mark with the correct numbers.

EXAMPLE

Problem: a. 1   b. 1, 2

 c. 1, 2, 3   d. ?

Answer: d. 1, 2, 3, 4

(What was done to part a to get part b? A comma was inserted, and the next number was listed. What was done to part b to get part c? The same thing—a comma, and then the next number. So to get part d, we do the same thing again—insert a comma and list the next number.)

PROBLEMS

212.

 a. 1   b. 3

 c. 9   d. 27

 e. ?

213.

 a. 123   b. 123456

 c. 123456789   d. ?

Reference

*Inductive
Thinking
Skills*

214.

    a. 28   b. 56

    c. 112   d. ?

215.

    a. 1234   b. 1243

    c. 1324   c. 1342

    e. 1423   f. ?

216.

    a. 12   b. 45

    c. 78   d. 1011

    e. ?

217.

    a. $\frac{1}{2}$ b. $\frac{3}{4}$

    c. $\frac{5}{6}$ d. ?

218.

    a. $\frac{3}{4}$ b. $\frac{1}{2}$

    c. $\frac{1}{3}$ d. $\frac{2}{9}$

    e. $\frac{4}{27}$ f. ?

Reference

*Math
Word
Problems*

SPEED OF LIGHT

LESSON

Some numbers are so large that they are almost meaningless to us because our minds can't grasp their immensity. For example, how far is 10,000,000,000,000 (ten trillion) miles?

Because of the stupendous distances they deal with, astronomers measure in *light-years* rather than in miles or kilometers.

A light-year is the distance light travels in a year at a speed of 186,281.7 miles a second.*

DIRECTIONS

If you compute with a calculator (or computer), use 186,281.7 miles a second for the speed of light, and use $365\frac{1}{4}$ days for a year. If you have to do everything by hand, use 186,000 miles a second and 365 days.

Problems

219. 1 kilometer = .6213712 miles

1 mile = 1.609344 kilometers

a. What is the speed of light in kilometers per second?

(If you are computing by hand, use 1 km = .6 mile or 1 mile = 1.6 km, whichever you need.)

b. Your answer has more significant digits than the problem had.

If you computed by hand, your answer should have no more than two significant digits. Otherwise, your answer should have no more than seven significant digits.

What are your new answers?

---

* This is the speed light travels in a vacuum. Interstellar space is so empty that any difference between actual speed and speed in a vacuum is not considered to be significant.

Reference

Math Word Problems

220. How many seconds are there in
a. an hour?

b. a day?

c. a year?

221. How far does light travel in
a. an hour?

b. a day?

c. a year?

222. How far is a light-year?

223. How long would it take a space ship traveling a million miles an hour to go one light-year?

Reference

Math
Word
Problems

224. Alpha Centauri is the star (other than our sun) that is the nearest to Earth.

Actually, Alpha Centauri is a cluster of three stars named Alpha Centauri A, Alpha Centauri B, and Alpha Centauri C.

Alpha Centauri C revolves around the other two.

Because it comes closer to our sun than either of the others, it is also called Proxima Centauri (the nearest star of Centaurus).

Proxima Centauri is about 4.3 light-years from us.

a. How many miles away from us is Proxima Centauri?

b. If Proxima Centauri exploded today, how long would it be before people on Earth could know about it?

Reference

*Math
Word
Problems*

225. The sun's distance from Earth varies from 91,400,000 miles to 94,500,000 miles, with a mean distance of 93,000,000 miles.

To the nearest whole minute and second, how long does it take light from the sun to reach Earth when the sun is

a. its shortest distance from Earth?

b. its longest distance from Earth?

c. its mean distance from Earth?

226. The moon's distance from Earth varies, but the mean distance is 238,857 miles.

The moon gives off no light of its own. The light that seems to come from the moon is light reflected from the sun.

To the nearest 1/4 second, how long does it take the reflected light from the moon to reach Earth?

(If you are computing by hand, use 239,000 miles for the moon's distance from Earth.)

Reference

Math
Word
Problems

INDEX OF REFRACTION

LESSON

Light does not travel through a medium (air or water, for instance) at the same speed as it travels in a vacuum.

To find the speed of light in a medium, we divide light's speed in a vacuum by a number called the *index of refraction* of the medium.

For example, if a medium has an index of refraction of $1\frac{1}{5}$, the speed of light through this medium would be (in miles per second) $186{,}000 \div 1\frac{1}{5} = 186{,}000 \div (6/5) = 186{,}000 \times \frac{5}{6} = 155{,}000$.

DIRECTIONS

For this problem, use 186,000 miles a second as the speed of light in a vacuum.

The problem tells you what the medium is and what the index of refraction is.

Find the speed of light in that medium. Give your answer to the nearest whole mile per second.

PROBLEM

227.   a. water; index of refraction $= 1\frac{3}{10}$

b. glass; index of refraction $= 1\frac{1}{2}$

c. diamond; index of refraction $= 2\frac{2}{5}$

Reference

Classroom Quickies, Books 1–3

REARRANGE LETTERS

DIRECTIONS

Use the letters at the top to fill in the chart so that words are formed and the sentence makes sense.

- A shaded space in the chart shows the end of a word.

- Except for the last line, the end of a line is not the end of a word unless there is a shaded space there.

- When you have filled in the chart, answer the question asked.

PROBLEM

228.

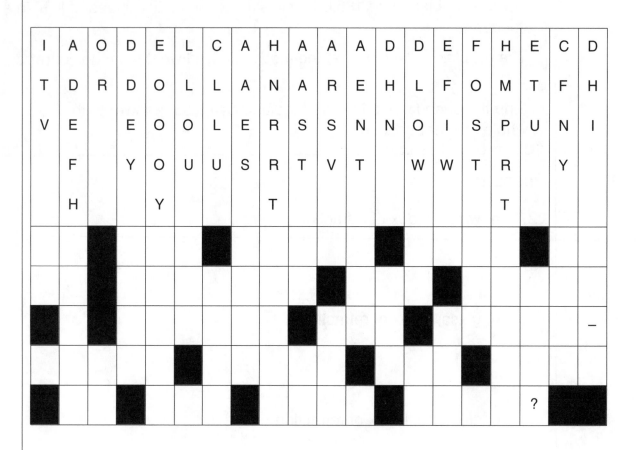

　© 1991, 1997 Critical Thinking Books & Software • P.O. Box 448, Pacific Grove, CA 93950 • 800-458-4849

Reference

Basic Thinking Skills

FOLLOWING DIRECTIONS

DIRECTIONS

Take a sheet of paper and a pencil (or pen).

Each part of the problem tells you to do something.

Do it all on the same sheet of paper.

PROBLEM

229. a. Write your name in the upper-right corner of your paper.

b. Do part c near the top of your paper. For the rest of the problem, print each new result under the previous result.

c. Print

IAMGOODLOOKINGBUT

d. Replace both letters in the second pair of look-alike vowels with *E*.

e. Duplicate the first two letters and tack on the duplications at the right end (in the same order).

f. Make three copies of the last consonant. Put one copy in the next-to-last position and one between each set of look-alike vowels.

g. Move the last letter so that it becomes the sixth letter from the end.

h. Make a copy of the eighth letter from the end. Replace the second and fifth consonants with the original and the copy.

i. Take the eighth letter from the right end and move it three positions to the left.

j. Change the fourth and fifth consonants from the right end to *C*. Move them so that one follows the third consonant and the other precedes the fifth vowel.

k. Move the fifth consonant from the left end so that it becomes the seventh letter from the right end.

l. Duplicate the third vowel (starting from the left end), and insert the duplication so that it is the fifth letter from the right end.

© 1991, 1997 Critical Thinking Books & Software • P.O. Box 448, Pacific Grove, CA 93950 • 800-458-4849

DRAWING INFERENCES

DIRECTIONS

Sometimes a problem needs only a "yes" or "no" answer, but be ready to tell why you chose your answer if you are asked about it.

Sometimes a problem doesn't tell you enough to let you know for sure what the answer is. In this case, answer "not enough information."

PROBLEMS

230. Gerald is older than Wilma but younger than Laurence.

Toby is younger than Wilma.

List the names in order, starting with the name of the oldest person.

231. A loaf of bread costs 40¢ more than an onion and 90¢ less than a pound of hamburger, which costs $1.69.

How much does each of the three items cost?

232. Serena wanted to go to a different school because she thought her present school had too many students.

Ken did not think his present school had too many students.

Did Serena and Ken go to the same school?

Reference

*Basic
Thinking
Skills*

*Math
Word
Problems*

MISCELLANEOUS PROBLEMS

PROBLEMS

233. A delicatessen sells imported cheese at $2.40 for a half-pound.

How much will three pounds of this cheese cost?

234. A medical doctor gives Ms. Dimitriou four pills and instructs her to take one every six hours starting now.

How long will it be before she takes the last of the pills?

Old tobogganers never die. They just go downhill.

Reference

Basic
Thinking
Skills

Algebra
Word
Problems—
Fun Time

235. Think of a number and write it down. Keep track of the results as you follow each new instruction.

Add 4 to the number.

Multiply by 6.

Subtract 18.

Divide by 3.

Multiply by 5.

Subtract 10.

Divide by 10.

The result is the number you started with. How come?

Rain sometimes brings rainbows, so why doesn't snow sometimes bring snowbows?

Reference

Basic
Thinking
Skills

236. A box contains exactly sixteen chess pawns, of which eight are black and eight are white.

The pawns are mixed up in the box so that they are not sorted by color.

Someone blindfolds you and tells you to start picking pawns out of the box. She says you can't look to see what color you're choosing.

What is the greatest number of pawns you'd have to take out of the box in order to know for sure (still without seeing them) that you had two pawns of

a. the same color? Explain.

b. different colors? Explain.

Michigan has more than 11,000 inland lakes and more than 36,000 miles of streams. How many does your state have?

Reference

*Basic
Thinking
Skills*

*Algebra
Word
Problems—
Fun Time*

237. Edwina telephones her grandmother once every five days and attends a skateboard club meeting once every two weeks.

Today she both telephoned her grandmother and attended a skateboard club meeting.

How long will it be before she again does both things on the same day?

Why does a firefighter wear red suspenders?

MATH MIND BENDERS®

LESSON

Your answers will be numbers. An answer might have one or more digits. Only one digit of an answer goes in a square.

Some of the squares in the grid are numbered so that they may be easily named.

"1-A" means that the answer starts in square 1 and reads across.

"4-D" means that the answer starts in square 4 and reads down.

1-A is a two-digit answer. (In the second grid 1-A is 47.) Two-digit answers also go in 1-D (45), 4-D (12), and 5-A (32).

One-digit answers go in 2-D (7), 3-A (5), 4-A (1), and 5-D (3).

As you can see, this kind of grid will take eight answers.

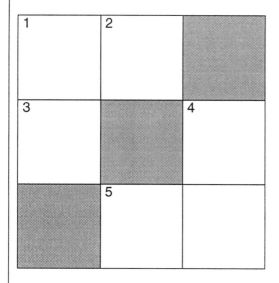

Reference

*Math
Mind
Benders®—
Warm Up*

DIRECTIONS

For each problem, copy the grid here and fill it in.

- You are given some of the answers to a problem. Arrange them so that they all fit into the grid. If you are given something like 3×4, find the product, 12, and fit 12 (not 3 and 4) into the grid.

- There may be more than one way to arrange the answers, but you need find only one way.

- If the answers you are given will not all fit into the grid, then tell why not.

PROBLEMS

238. $168 \div 2$; $3^2 + 37$; $(12 + 16) \div 2$; the product of 6 and 7

239. For this problem, you are told where one of the answers must go.

$2^2 \times 3^2$; 3×7; $6 \times 5 - 1$; 20 more than 4-D

240. 47, 46, 43, 49

LESSON CONT.

Here is a sample problem. You will see that a short story is followed by clues that tell you where the answers go. No answer begins with 0.

You will not necessarily be able to fill in the answers in the same order as the clues are given.

SAMPLE PROBLEM

Ramona is 2 years older than Bernice, who is 3 years older than Horace. Ramona's great-aunt Martha is a jet pilot.

ACROSS	DOWN
1. Age of Pat, Ramona's sister	1. Ramona's age
3. Test problems Ramona got wrong yesterday	2. Horace's age
4. Bernice's age	4. Age of Great-aunt Martha's father
5. 4 × half of 1-A	5. Age of Spot, Ramona's cat

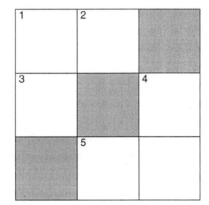

Only clues 4-A, 1-D, and 2-D are connected with the story. Notice that 1-D is a two-digit answer, and 4-A is a one-digit answer.

1-D is 2 more than 4-A (given in the story), so 1-D must be 10 or 11. If 1-D were 10, then 3-A would be 0, which is forbidden. So 1-D is 11, and 4-A is 9. Then 2-D is 6.

Reference

Math Mind Benders®— Warm Up & Warm Up-2

Here is the sample problem again, along with what we have filled in so far.

SAMPLE PROBLEM

Ramona is 2 years older than Bernice, who is 3 years older than Horace. Ramona's great-aunt Martha is a jet pilot.

ACROSS	DOWN
1. Age of Pat, Ramona's sister	1. Ramona's age
3. Test problems Ramona got wrong yesterday	2. Horace's age
4. Bernice's age	4. Age of Great-aunt Martha's father
5. 4 × half of 1-A	5. Age of Spot, Ramona's cat

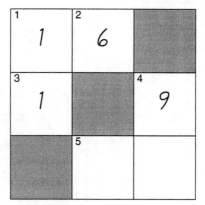

Now go to clue 5-A, which says to take 4 × half of 1-A. Half of 1-A is 8. Then 4 × 8 = 32, so 5-A is 32.

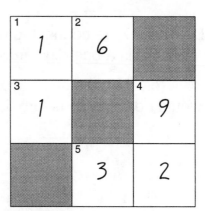

All squares are filled in now. We go back and read the clues we have ignored until now, in order to make sure there are no contradictions. These are clues 1-A, 3-A, 4-D, and 5-D. In each case, the answer is suitable.

Reference

Math Mind Benders®— Book A–1

DIRECTIONS

In the clues, "A" means across, and "D" means down. For example, "4-D" would refer to clue number 4 DOWN.

Each square takes a single digit from 0 through 9. No answer begins with 0.

PROBLEM

241. Jane is 2 years older than Carla, who is 5 years younger than Ann. Jane's great-aunt Martha is a safari leader in Africa.

ACROSS
1. Age of Great-aunt Martha's pet dik-dik
2. Ann's age
4. 8-D ÷ 5
6. Age of Great-aunt Martha's pet parrot
7. (9-A + 6-A) × 10-A
9. Jane's age
10. Great-aunt Martha's age

DOWN
1. 2-A × 3-D × 11-D
2. Years until Great-aunt Martha's retirement
3. Jane's age 10 years from now
5. Age of Great-aunt Martha's oldest niece
8. Age of Wolfe, Great-aunt Martha's husband
11. Carla's age

1		2	3
4	5		6
7		8	
9		10	11

Reference

Math Mind Benders®— Book A–1

DIRECTIONS

In the clues, "A" means across, and "D" means down. For example, "4-D" would refer to clue number 4 DOWN.

Each square takes a single digit from 0 through 9. No answer begins with 0.

PROBLEM

242. Kerry found that when he adds consecutive numbers starting with 1, the sum is always half the product of the last number and the number after it.

ACROSS	DOWN
1. Age of Lauren, Kerry's youngest sister	1. Sum of numbers 1-138, inclusive
2. 11-D × sum of digits of 7-A	2. 1-A – 11-D
4. 2-A + 11-D	3. Kerry's age (= 10-A – 9-A)
6. Years Kerry's great-aunt Martha has had a paper route	5. Age of Great-aunt Martha
7. 1-D ÷ (3-D × 6-A), with answer digits reversed	8. Strikeouts by Kerry in his last game pitched last summer
9. First digit of 8-D	11. Years of college Kerry completed
10. Sum of digits of 1-D	

1		2	3
4	5		6
7		8	
9		10	11

References

Algebra
Word
Problems—
Diophantine
Problems

Classroom
Quickies,
Books 1—
3

DIOPHANTINE PROBLEMS

PROBLEM

243. Angelica and Morton washed more walls and are going to another garage sale with another $100.

T-shirts are $2 each, blouses are $4 each, and socks are 2 pairs for $1.

If they buy 100 items with their $100, how many of each will they get? (Count a pair of socks as one item.)

(Hint: There are five different answers to this problem.)

Why did the little kid expect to find artists inside the dresser?

References

Classroom Quickies, Books 1–3

WATER JUGS PROBLEMS

PROBLEMS

244. You have three jugs and a river of clean water.

The jugs are known to hold exactly 3, 7, and 10 liters.

Tell how you can use these jugs to measure exactly 5 liters of water.

Aside from zoos, the kangaroo is found only in Australia.

245. You have been given, so far, a total of three problems in which you were given three jugs of varying capacities and were asked how to use them to get a certain amount of water.

In each case, the capacity of at least one of the jugs was an odd number.

Now suppose you are given three jugs, and suppose the capacity of each one is an even number of liters.

Explain why you can't get an end result of an odd number of liters.

Does the answer change if the capacities of the jugs are in quarts instead of liters? How come?

The adult male of some species of kangaroo stands an average of six feet tall, but a newborn baby kangaroo is only about one *inch* long.

Reference

Math
Word
Problems

MISCELLANEOUS PROBLEMS

PROBLEMS

246. Ms. Harvey owns a small dress store. She needs to attract more customers in order to earn a living from the store.

She knows that people buy items more readily if they believe they are getting bargains, so she thinks of a way to charge her normal prices and yet make the customers think they are buying at a discount.

What she will do is this: after attaching new price tags, she will put a large sign in the window saying, "SALE! 1 week only! 1/3 off all tagged prices!"

In other words, she will increase each normal price by enough so that when 1/3 of the new price is subtracted from the new price, the result is the normal price.

a. If the normal price of a dress is $20, what will the new tagged price be, and how much (in $) will the discount be on this new price?

b. By what fraction of the normal price will the normal price be increased in order to compute the new tagged price?

c. Instead of taking some fraction of the normal price and adding the result to that price (in order to get the new tagged price), the normal price can simply be multiplied by some number. (This multiplier is not a whole number.) What is this multiplier?

Reference

*Math
Word
Problems*

247. If eight typists can type eight pages in eight minutes,

    a. how many minutes will it take sixteen typists to type sixteen pages?

    b. how many typists will it take to type sixteen pages in sixteen minutes?

    c. how many pages can sixteen typists type in sixteen minutes?

REPLACE THE LETTERS

DIRECTIONS

Replace each letter with one of the digits from 0–9.

- A letter that appears more than once is to be replaced with the same digit each time it appears.

- Two different letters will not represent the same digit.

- One of the digits has been filled in for you.

PROBLEM

248.

```
      R O S E
   +    R E D
            3
   S C E N T
```

The Grand Canyon National Park in northwestern Arizona has 90 kinds of animals and 180 kinds of birds.

MISCELLANEOUS PROBLEMS

PROBLEMS

249. Hvid Gjetost is a Norwegian goat's-milk cheese.

If a Norwegian goat costs $100, how much will 5 pounds of Hvid Gjetost at $3.50 a pound cost?

250. a. In the U.S., if there are about 325 million egg-laying chickens, and if these chickens produce about 75 billion eggs a year, to the nearest whole number how many eggs per chicken is that (on the average)?

b. If 25,000,000 chickens each lay half an egg a day, and if it takes three eggs to make an omelet, how many omelets can be made from the eggs the chickens lay in six days, and what color are the majority of the chickens?

Reference

Classroom Quickies, Books 1–3

REARRANGE LETTERS

DIRECTIONS

Use the letters at the top to fill in the chart so that words are formed and the sentence makes sense.

- A shaded space in the chart shows the end of a word.

- Except for the last line, the end of a line is not the end of a word unless there is a shaded space there.

- When you have filled in the chart, answer the question asked.

PROBLEM

251.

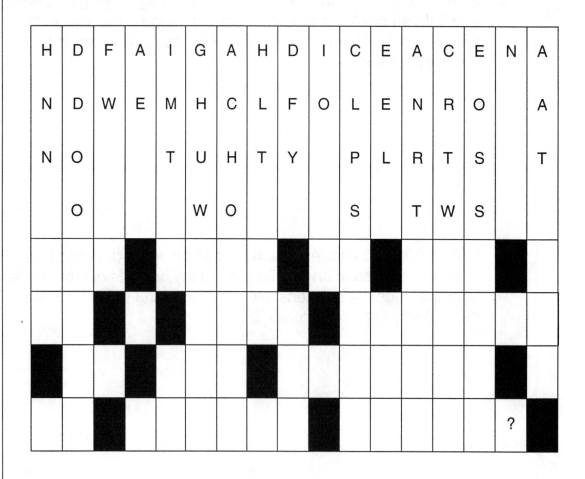

© 1991, 1997 Critical Thinking Books & Software • P.O. Box 448, Pacific Grove, CA 93950 • 800-458-4849

Reference

*Math
Word
Problems*

MISCELLANEOUS PROBLEMS

PROBLEM

252. A game was played in which words were to be made from seven given letters.

During one part of the game, double points were given for the first letter, and triple points for the fourth letter, of any word formed.

Gregory and Leila both played and both used all seven letters for their words, but their first and fourth letters were switched.

Gregory's first letter was *H* (usually 4 points) and his fourth letter was *C* (usually 2 points), while Leila's were the opposite.

Whose word was worth more, and how much more? (Or isn't enough information given for you to tell?)

If 14 + 35 = 52, what number base is being used?

Reference

Taken from *Mind Benders®— B3*

MIND BENDERS®

PROBLEMS

253. Allan, Daphne, Eunice, and Howard, whose last names are Franklin, Jackson, Kingsley, and Lohmer, created quite a stir when they took their pets (buffalo, cheetah, vulture, zebra) to school for "show and tell." The colors of the pets' collars are green, red, white, and yellow.

Match up everything from the clues below.

a. The buffalo has a yellow collar.

b. Howard's pet does not have a green collar.

c. Neither Eunice's pet nor Franklin's pet flies or has a green collar.

d. Neither Daphne's nor Kingsley's pet has feathers or is spotted.

e. Neither Allan's pet nor the pet with the red collar has a beak.

f. The striped animal, which is the pet of neither Eunice nor Jackson, doesn't have a red collar.

Reference

Taken from *Mind Benders®— B3*

Chart for problem 253

	Franklin	Jackson	Kingsley	Lohmer	buffalo	cheetah	vulture	zebra	green	red	white	yellow
Allan												
Daphne												
Eunice												
Howard												
buffalo												
cheetah												
vulture												
zebra												
green												
red												
white												
yellow												

254. Bernard, Dorothy, Edwin, Faith, and Jeannine, whose last names are Casey, Gardner, Hooper, Kulper, and Martin, have favorite drinks for hot weather (apple juice, iced tea, lemonade, orange juice, pineapple juice).

Match up the names and drinks from the clues below.

a. Hooper doesn't like apple juice.

b. Gardner doesn't like lemonade.

c. The person whose favorite drink is orange juice, who isn't Dorothy, gets along well with everyone.

d. Jeannine likes all the drinks, but she likes one, which isn't iced tea or orange juice, the best.

e. Edwin and Martin don't get along well with the person whose favorite drink is lemonade, who isn't Casey.

f. Martin and Jeannine and the person whose favorite drink is apple juice are good friends.

g. Aside from one other person, Bernard doesn't get along well with anyone.

h. Casey doesn't like some of the drinks, but she likes at least two of them.

Reference

Taken from *Mind Benders®— B4*

Chart for problem 254

	Casey	Gardner	Hooper	Kulper	Martin	apple juice	iced tea	lemonade	orange juice	pineapple juice
Bernard										
Dorothy										
Edwin										
Faith										
Jeannine										
apple juice										
iced tea										
lemonade										
orange juice										
pineapple juice										

DRAWING INFERENCES

DIRECTIONS

Sometimes a problem needs only a "yes" or "no" answer, but be ready to tell why you chose your answer if you are asked about it.

Sometimes a problem doesn't tell you enough to let you know for sure what the answer is. In this case, answer "not enough information."

PROBLEMS

255. Pasquale had more problems right on today's test than Neil had right on yesterday's test.

Marnie had more problems right on yesterday's test than Pasquale had right on today's test.

Did Marnie have more problems right on yesterday's test than Pasquale had right on today's test?

256. Beef costs less than veal but more than pork.

Turkey costs more than chicken but less than pork.

List the five kinds of meat, starting with the least expensive.

257. Ty Smith is a medical doctor.

Tyler Smith is a psychiatrist.

Can Ty Smith and Tyler Smith be the same person?

Reference

*Math
Word
Problems*

MISCELLANEOUS PROBLEMS

PROBLEMS

258. A rainfall of 1 inch = a dry fluffy snowfall of 30 inches.
a-c. How many inches of rainfall would = a dry fluffy snowfall of

   a. 25 inches?

   b. 12 inches?

   c. $1\frac{1}{2}$ feet?

d-g. How many feet of dry fluffy snowfall would = a rainfall of

   d. $1\frac{1}{2}$ inches?

   e. 3/4 inch?

   f. 1/24 foot?

   g. 1.2 inches?

MISCELLANEOUS PROBLEMS

PROBLEMS

259. The number of hairs on the human head can be anywhere from 0 through 200,000.

Prove that at least two people in Chicago have exactly the same number of hairs on their heads (as each other).

In the fairy tale, what was Hansel and Gretel's last name?

© 1991, 1997 Critical Thinking Books & Software • P.O. Box 448, Pacific Grove, CA 93950 • 800-458-4849

Reference

*Math
Word
Problems*

260. The formula to find a circle's circumference is $C = \pi d$.

Assume the earth is a perfect sphere and its circumference is 25,000 miles. Imagine that we have a (long!) belt that fits exactly around the earth at the equator.

Now suppose we lengthen the belt by 20 feet and distribute this extra length equally around the equator. (So the belt will no longer touch the ground at any point.)

Take a guess at how much room there will be between the belt and the ground now. (Enough to slide a piece of paper between? Enough to slide a finger between? Enough to crawl under? Enough to walk under? Or what?)

Now figure out how much room there will really be.

Handbooks used by engineers usually give π to at least ten places, 3.1415926536. For practical purposes, this is so accurate that if Earth's diameter were 8,000 miles, the difference between using π to ten places and π to eleven places to figure Earth's circumference would make a difference of less than $\frac{1}{100}$ inch. (π to eleven places is 3.14159265359.)

261. The country of Nurgarden issues only two kinds of postage stamps—7¢ and 10¢.

Obviously, there is no way to combine the stamps to get some amounts—for instance, 2¢ or 23¢ or 36¢.

What is the *highest* amount of postage that these stamps cannot be combined to make?

P.S. The country of Nurgarden shouldn't sound familiar to you, because I made up the name.

Reference

*Math
Word
Problems*

What did the initial *S* stand for in Harry S. Truman's name?

Reference

Critical Thinking, Book 1

DRAWING INFERENCES

PROBLEM

262. Norman and Catherine go to different schools in the same city.

Norman's school cafeteria charges more for a meal than Catherine's school cafeteria charges, but the meals at Norman's school are smaller.

Give logical reasons that might account for this.

What did the initial *S* stand for in Ulysses S. Grant's name?

DIOPHANTINE PROBLEMS

PROBLEM

263. Angelica and Morton mowed lawns this time to earn their $100.

They've had so much fun going to garage sales that they've decided to go to another one.

They've found a good set of tires for $40, some computer games for $6 each, shirts at $4 each, and a boxful of odds and ends priced at 5 for $1.

How many of each will they get if they buy 100 items with their $100?

(Hint: There are two different answers to this problem.

The question does not imply that they have to buy some of each of the four items named.)

DRAWING INFERENCES

DIRECTIONS

Sometimes a problem needs only a "yes" or "no" answer, but be ready to tell why you chose your answer if you are asked about it.

Sometimes a problem doesn't tell you enough to let you know for sure what the answer is. In this case, answer "not enough information."

PROBLEMS

264. Mr. Lenka never had any children.

Jeannette has a grandfather.

Can Mr. Lenka be Jeannette's grandfather?

265. Mr. Menton doesn't have any children.

Mary has a grandfather.

Can Mr. Menton be Mary's grandfather?

266. Anita telephoned Frances, who told her, "I was sleeping, and the telephone woke me up just now."

Anita said, "I've been awake for an hour."

Both girls woke up at 6:30 A.M.

Can both girls be telling the truth? Explain.

MISCELLANEOUS PROBLEMS

PROBLEM

267. Mr. Portman points to a pork loin 10" long and tells the butcher he wants only half of it.

The butcher slices the pork loin so that there are two parts, each 5" long, and returns one of the parts to the meat counter.

Mr. Portman then says he wants his half of the loin sliced into smaller parts so that, instead of one long 5" piece, he will have several smaller pieces, each 1/2" long.

The butcher does as Mr. Portman has directed.

a. How many pieces does Mr. Portman end up with?

b. How many times did the butcher have to slice the pork loin, not counting the time it was sliced in half (to reduce it from 10" to 5" in length)?

Who invented bifocal lenses for eyeglasses?

References

Classroom Quickies, Books 1–3

WATER JUGS PROBLEMS

PROBLEM

268. You have two jugs and a spring of clear water.

The jugs are known to hold exactly 7 and 5 liters.

Tell how you can use these jugs to measure exactly 6 liters of water.

If dark clouds bring rain, then why isn't the rain they bring dark?

ANALOGIES IN PROPORTIONS

LESSON

A fraction is a *ratio* (RAY sho).

A *true* statement that two ratios are equal is a *proportion* (pruh POR shun).

We say that two equal ratios are *proportional* or *in proportion* to each other.

EXAMPLES 1

These are ratios:

$$\frac{1}{2} \qquad \frac{5}{3} \qquad \frac{243}{5716} \qquad \frac{5716}{243}$$

These are proportions:

$$\frac{1}{2} = \frac{3}{6} \qquad \frac{2}{1} = \frac{6}{3} \qquad \frac{48}{150} = \frac{8}{25}$$

These are proportional, and they are in proportion to each other:

$$\frac{2}{1} \text{ and } \frac{10}{5} \qquad \frac{3}{5} \text{ and } \frac{6}{10}$$

To show that two ratios do *not* form a proportion, we strike a bar slantwise (/) through the equal sign (=) and get ≠.

EXAMPLES 2

It is false to say $\frac{1}{2} = \frac{2}{3}$, so instead we write $\frac{1}{2} \neq \frac{2}{3}$.

$\frac{1}{3}$ is not in proportion to $\frac{2}{3}$, so $\frac{1}{3} \neq \frac{2}{3}$.

$\frac{2}{3}$ is not proportional to $\frac{2}{5}$, so $\frac{2}{3} \neq \frac{2}{5}$.

These pairs of ratios are shown to be nonproportional:

$$\frac{1}{2} \neq \frac{2}{6} \qquad \frac{2}{1} \neq \frac{6}{4} \qquad \frac{48}{150} \neq \frac{8}{21}$$

A proportion can be stated as an analogy.

EXAMPLES 3

$\frac{1}{2} = \frac{3}{6}$, so 1 is to 2 as 3 is to 6.

$\frac{48}{150} = \frac{8}{25}$, so 48 is to 150 as 8 is to 25.

Notice that an analogy uses "is to" instead of a fraction bar (—) and uses "as" instead of an equal sign (=). So, given the proportion

$$\frac{2}{4} = \frac{5}{10}$$

an analogy reads it as

2 is to 4 as 5 is to 10

instead of

two fourths equals five tenths

and instead of

2 divided by 4 equals 5 divided by 10.

If two ratios are nonproportional, an analogy cannot be formed from them. Conversely, if an analogy cannot be formed from two ratios, then the ratios are not proportional.

EXAMPLES 4

$\frac{1}{2} \neq \frac{3}{5}$, so it is false that 1 is to 2 as 3 is to 5.

It is not true that 2 is to 3 as 4 is to 7, so $\frac{2}{3} \neq \frac{4}{7}$.

> **DIRECTIONS**
>
> You are given four numbers.
>
> Tell whether or not they can be used to form a proportion.
>
> If they can, then use them to write at least three different proportions.
>
> Also state each proportion as an analogy.

EXAMPLE 1

Problem: 4, 5, 2, 10

Answer: Yes.

$\frac{4}{2} = \frac{10}{5}$; 4 is to 2 as 10 is to 5

$\frac{2}{5} = \frac{4}{10}$; 2 is to 5 as 4 is to 10

$\frac{2}{4} = \frac{5}{10}$; 2 is to 4 as 5 is to 10

(There are also five other proportions that can be made from these four numbers.)

EXAMPLE 2

Problem: 1, 5, 2, 8

Answer: No.

PROBLEMS

269. 1, 4, 2, 8

270. 4, 3, 1, 12

271. 5, 1, 2, 4

272. 9, 2, 18, 4

273. 3, 16, 4, 12

274. 6, 25, 10, 15

275. 5, 10, 24, 12

276. 7, 14, 21, 35

Hints for Problems on pages 157–175

If a problem talks about a common factor, assume that this factor is not 1. Also assume that all numbers are greater than zero.

If you are not given any numbers, find numbers of your own to use. See how they relate to each other or what happens to them when you do what the problem says.

Then choose another set of numbers. See if they relate to each other or act in the same way as the first numbers did.

Keep choosing numbers until you can *predict* what they have to be like or what will happen to them in the problem. (Or maybe you feel that *no* numbers will work.) Figure out how to prove that your reasoning would apply no matter which (allowable) numbers were chosen.

You are allowed to use anything already proved. For example, if you are doing problem 285 and need to use a statement proved in problem 281, then you may do so without proving it again.

To help yourself imagine a general proportion, make a set of fraction bars and an equal sign

$$\text{—} = \text{—}$$

and fill in the four terms with four different geometric figures—say, a circle, a square, a triangle, and a rhombus:

$$\frac{\bigcirc}{\square} = \frac{\triangle}{\didiagup\!\diagup}$$

Then you'll have something to stare at while you're trying to figure out how to solve the problem.

277. Someone is thinking of a proportion in which three of the four numbers are the same.

What, if anything, can you tell about the remaining number without actually seeing the proportion? How come?

278. You are given a proportion.

Prove that you can switch the two ratios (to the opposite sides of the equation) and still have a proportion.

279. You are given four numbers that can be the terms of a proportion.

Tell how many different proportions are possible, and give an example of such a proportion, if

a. two of the numbers are the same, and the other two are different from those

    1) but the same as each other

    2) and from each other

b. the four numbers are distinct

© 1991, 1997 Critical Thinking Books & Software • P.O. Box 448, Pacific Grove, CA 93950 • 800-458-4849

LESSON

If you can understand how an *indirect proof* works, you will have a powerful mathematical tool available for use.

The steps for an indirect proof are these:

Step 1. Take the *opposite* of what is to be proved, and suppose it is true.

Step 2. Follow through until a contradiction is reached.

Step 3. Conclude that the supposition has to be wrong.

EXAMPLE

Problem: Prove that if one ratio in a proportion has a value of 1, then the other ratio also has a value of 1.

(Indirect) Proof: Suppose the second ratio is not worth 1. Then the two ratios are unequal, and so they cannot be proportional. This is a contradiction because we are given a proportion. Therefore, our supposition has to be wrong, and so the second ratio has a value of 1.

Now try using an indirect proof on the problem below.

Problem

280. You are given two ratios that are proportional.

One of the ratios has two unequal terms.

Prove that the terms of the other ratio are also unequal.

281. You are given a proportion. Prove the following:

    a. If the numerators are equal, then the denominators are equal.

    b. If the denominators are equal, then the numerators are equal.

    c. Even if you hadn't been told (at the start of this series of problems) that none of our numbers would be zero, the denominators would have to be nonzero.

LESSON CONT.

A proportion always looks like this:

$$\frac{\text{first term}}{\text{second term}} = \frac{\text{third term}}{\text{fourth term}}$$

The first and fourth terms are called the *extremes*, or the outer terms, of the proportion.

The second and third terms are called the *means*, or the inner terms, of the proportion.

PROBLEM

282. You are given a proportion.

Prove that the product of the extremes equals the product of the means.

Here are two other ways to state what you are to prove:

first term × fourth term = second term × third term

product of outer terms = product of inner terms

Here is a list of some of the problems proved. If a statement says you can do something to a proportion, then you will still have a proportion afterwards. In this list, GAP = Given a proportion.

281. GAP, if the numerators are =, then the denominators are =; if the denominators are =, then the numerators are =.

282. GAP, the product of the extremes = the product of the means.

283. Prove that a proportion cannot have 1, 2, 3, and 4 as its four terms, no matter in what order they are used.

Here is a list of some of the problems proved. If a statement says you can do something to a proportion, then you will still have a proportion afterwards. In this list, GAP = Given a proportion.

281. GAP, if the numerators are =, then the denominators are =; if the denominators are =, then the numerators are =.

282. GAP, the product of the extremes = the product of the means.

284. You are given that the product of two numbers equals the product of two other numbers. (For example, $3 \times 4 = 2 \times 6$.)

Prove that a proportion will be formed if you use one pair of numbers as the extremes and the other pair as the means.

Explain why it doesn't matter which pair you choose for the extremes.

EXAMPLE

Given $3 \times 4 = 2 \times 6$, suppose you choose 3 and 4 to be the extremes. Then 2 and 6 will be the means, and the proportion could look like this:

$$\frac{3}{2} = \frac{6}{4}$$

Or if you choose 2 and 6 to be the extremes, then 3 and 4 will be the means, and your proportion could look like this:

$$\frac{2}{3} = \frac{4}{6}$$

(Hint: You are given an equation. Remember that both sides of an equation can be divided by the same number.)

Here is a list of some of the problems proved. If a statement says you can do something to a proportion, then you will still have a proportion afterwards. In this list, GAP = Given a proportion.

281. GAP, if the numerators are =, then the denominators are =; if the denominators are =, then the numerators are =.

282. GAP, the product of the extremes = the product of the means.

284. If the product of two numbers = the product of two numbers, then either pair may be made the extremes of a proportion, and the other pair will be the means.

285. You are given a proportion. Prove that you will still have a proportion if you switch
a. the means of the given proportion

b. the extremes of the given proportion

Note: The new proportions will be different from the old proportion.

Here is a list of some of the problems proved. If a statement says you can do something to a proportion, then you will still have a proportion afterwards. In this list, GAP = Given a proportion.

281. GAP, if the numerators are =, then the denominators are =; if the denominators are =, then the numerators are =.

282. GAP, the product of the extremes = the product of the means.

284. If the product of two numbers = the product of two numbers, then either pair may be made the extremes of a proportion, and the other pair will be the means.

285. GAP, the means can be switched, and so can the extremes.

286. You are given a proportion.

Prove that if you invert both of the proportion's ratios (turn them both upside down), the result will still be a proportion.

Here is a list of some of the problems proved. If a statement says you can do something to a proportion, then you will still have a proportion afterwards. In this list, GAP = Given a proportion.

281. GAP, if the numerators are =, then the denominators are =; if the denominators are =, then the numerators are =.

282. GAP, the product of the extremes = the product of the means.

284. If the product of two numbers = the product of two numbers, then either pair may be made the extremes of a proportion, and the other pair will be the means.

285. GAP, the means can be switched, and so can the extremes.

286. GAP, the ratios can be inverted.

287. Suppose you have a proportion that has four distinct terms, and suppose you switch two of the terms.

Answer questions A–C for each part of the problem (items a–f) below.

   A. Will you still have a proportion?

   B. If so, how come?

   C. If not, will you have a proportion if you also switch the other two terms. If so, how come?

TERMS YOU SWITCH

   a.   first and second terms

   b.   first and third terms

   c.   first and fourth terms

   d.   second and third terms

   e.   second and fourth terms

   f.   third and fourth terms

Here is a list of some of the problems proved. If a statement says you can do something to a proportion, then you will still have a proportion afterwards. In this list, GAP = Given a proportion.

281. GAP, if the numerators are =, then the denominators are =; if the denominators are =, then the numerators are =.

282. GAP, the product of the extremes = the product of the means.

284. If the product of two numbers = the product of two numbers, then either pair may be made the extremes of a proportion, and the other pair will be the means.

285. GAP, the means can be switched, and so can the extremes.

286. GAP, the ratios can be inverted.

288. You are given four numbers that will be terms of a proportion if you can place them correctly.

Prove that a proportion can be formed no matter which one of the four numbers you use as the first term, if

a. two of the numbers are the same, and the other two numbers are

    1) the same as each other but different from the first two

    2) different from each other and from the first two

b. the four numbers are distinct

Here is a list of some of the problems proved. If a statement says you can do something to a proportion, then you will still have a proportion afterwards. In this list, GAP = Given a proportion.

281. GAP, if the numerators are =, then the denominators are =; if the denominators are =, then the numerators are =.

282. GAP, the product of the extremes = the product of the means.

284. If the product of two numbers = the product of two numbers, then either pair may be made the extremes of a proportion, and the other pair will be the means.

285. GAP, the means can be switched, and so can the extremes.

286. GAP, the ratios can be inverted.

288. If a proportion can be formed from four numbers, then any one of the numbers can be the first term.

289. You are given four distinct numbers that can be the four terms of a proportion.

Prove that the numbers can be sorted in at least two ways so that a proportion is *not* formed.

Here is a list of some of the problems proved. If a statement says you can do something to a proportion, then you will still have a proportion afterwards. In this list, GAP = Given a proportion.

281. GAP, if the numerators are =, then the denominators are =; if the denominators are =, then the numerators are =.

282. GAP, the product of the extremes = the product of the means.

284. If the product of two numbers = the product of two numbers, then either pair may be made the extremes of a proportion, and the other pair will be the means.

285. GAP, the means can be switched, and so can the extremes.

286. GAP, the ratios can be inverted.

288. If a proportion can be formed from four numbers, then any one of the numbers can be the first term.

290. You are given four numbers that can be arranged to form a proportion.

Prove that you can start the arrangement by choosing any one of the four numbers for any one of the four terms of a proportion.

Here is a list of some of the problems proved. If a statement says you can do something to a proportion, then you will still have a proportion afterwards. In this list, GAP = Given a proportion.

284. If the product of two numbers = the product of two numbers, then either pair may be made the extremes of a proportion, and the other pair will be the means.

290. If a proportion can be formed from four numbers, then any number chosen first can be used for any of the four terms.

291. You are given four numbers.

For each of the special conditions listed below (a, b, and c), tell whether or not it is possible to arrange the four numbers to form a proportion.

In each case,

A. if a proportion is possible, give an example of such a proportion. You are allowed to use any numbers you choose for this.

B. if a proportion is not possible, tell why not.

EXAMPLE

Special condition: One of the numbers is five more than another of the numbers.

Answer: Yes. $\frac{1}{6} = \frac{2}{12}$ (Other proportions are possible.)

SPECIAL CONDITIONS FOR THE PROBLEM

a. One of the terms is a proper fraction, but the other three are distinct whole numbers.

b. Two of the terms are proper fractions, and the other two are distinct whole numbers.

> Here is a list of some of the problems proved. If a statement says you can do something to a proportion, then you will still have a proportion afterwards. In this list, GAP = Given a proportion.
>
> **282.** GAP, the product of the extremes = the product of the means.
>
> **285.** GAP, the means can be switched, and so can the extremes.
>
> **286.** GAP, the ratios can be inverted.
>
> **290.** If a proportion can be formed from four numbers, then any number chosen first can be used for any of the four terms.

292. You are given four distinct whole numbers (none of which are 1) and are told to organize them into a proportion.

a. Can this possibly be done if three of the numbers have a common factor but the other number does not have this factor?

If so, give an example of such a proportion. If not, explain why not.

b. Suppose no two of these numbers have a common factor.

Prove that it is not possible to use the numbers to form a proportion.

Here is a list of some of the problems proved. If a statement says you can do something to a proportion, then you will still have a proportion afterwards. In this list, GAP = Given a proportion.

282. GAP, the product of the extremes = the product of the means.

285. GAP, the means can be switched, and so can the extremes.

286. GAP, the ratios can be inverted.

288. If a proportion can be formed from four numbers, then any one of the numbers can be the first term.

292. Given four distinct whole numbers such that no two have a common factor, a proportion cannot be formed.

293. You are given four numbers and you don't know whether or not they can be positioned to form a proportion.

PROVE:

a. If you choose a number as the first term, then you need to try at most two of the three remaining numbers as the second term in order to decide whether or not a proportion can be formed.

b. If you don't get a proportion from part a above, then a proportion can't be formed even if you choose a different first term.

Here is a list of some of the problems proved. If a statement says you can do something to a proportion, then you will still have a proportion afterwards. In this list, GAP = Given a proportion.

282. GAP, the product of the extremes = the product of the means.

285. GAP, the means can be switched, and so can the extremes.

286. GAP, the ratios can be inverted.

290. If a proportion can be formed from four numbers, then any number chosen first can be used for any of the four terms.

293. If you've chosen one of four numbers as the first term of a potential proportion, and if two of the other three numbers don't work as a second term, then a proportion can't be formed.

294. You have four numbers and you decide to see if they can form a proportion. You choose two of them—one for the first term and one for the second term. You use the other two numbers as the third and fourth terms, but you don't get a proportion. You switch the last two terms and still don't get a proportion.

a. Might you get a proportion if you switch the first and second terms? If so, give an example of such a case. If not, tell why not.

b. You intend to try again, so you keep the same first term, but you choose a different second term.

   1) Is that really necessary? (You didn't get a proportion using the number you first chose as the second term, so wasn't that enough to show that the four numbers will not form a proportion?) Explain.

   2) If you think you should try a different second term, what if this one doesn't work, either? You will have tested two of the three numbers available. Will that last number have to be tested, too? Explain.

c. Could your answers to the questions above change if you happened to choose a different one of the given numbers as the first term? Explain.

Here is a list of some of the problems proved. If a statement says you can do something to a proportion, then you will still have a proportion afterwards. In this list, GAP = Given a proportion.

282. GAP, the product of the extremes = the product of the means.

285. GAP, the means can be switched, and so can the extremes.

286. GAP, the ratios can be inverted.

290. If a proportion can be formed from four numbers, then any number chosen first can be used for any of the four terms.

292. Given four distinct whole numbers such that no two have a common factor, a proportion cannot be formed.

295. You have a proportion whose terms are distinct whole numbers.

Prove that at least one pair of terms have a common factor and that another pair of terms also have a common factor.

The two common factors may or may not be the same number.

(Hint 1: The problem doesn't say you can't have the same term in both pairs.

The four terms can be paired in six distinct ways.

For example, one pair would be the first and second terms, and another pair would be the first and third terms.

Hint 2: Consider these possibilities: What if one of the terms is 1? What if it isn't? What if one of the terms is a multiple of another? What if it isn't?)

Here is a list of some of the problems proved. If a statement says you can do something to a proportion, then you will still have a proportion afterwards. In this list, GAP = Given a proportion.

281. GAP, if the numerators are =, then the denominators are =; if the denominators are =, then the numerators are =.

282. GAP, the product of the extremes = the product of the means.

284. If the product of two numbers = the product of two numbers, then either pair may be made the extremes of a proportion, and the other pair will be the means.

295. GAP whose terms are distinct whole numbers, at least two pairs of terms have common factors.

296. * EXTRA CREDIT *

You are given two ratios whose terms are distinct whole numbers.

a. Suppose there is a number that is a factor of at least one term in both ratios.

Prove that this is not enough to make the ratios proportional.

b. Suppose there is no number that is a factor of at least one term in both ratios. (That is, no factor of the first term is also a factor of the third or fourth term. Likewise, no factor of the second term is also a factor of the third or fourth term.)

Prove the two ratios are not proportional.

(Hint for part b: Try using an indirect proof.)

DRAWING INFERENCES

DIRECTIONS

Sometimes a problem needs only a "yes" or "no" answer, but be ready to tell why you chose your answer if you are asked about it.

Sometimes a problem doesn't tell you enough to let you know for sure what the answer is. In this case, answer "not enough information."

PROBLEMS

297. A gromyx is more than either a lemip or an orlib.

An orlib is less than either a fanig or a lemip.

A cunir is more than a gromyx.

A fanig is less than a lemip.

List the five things in order, starting with the least.

298. Gin-Eing does not have any sisters.

Gin-Chang does not have any brothers.

a. Can Gin-Eing be Gin-Chang's sister?

b. Can Gin-Chang be Gin-Eing's brother?

Reference

Classroom Quickies, Books 1– 3

REARRANGE LETTERS

DIRECTIONS

Use the letters at the top to fill in the chart so that words are formed and the sentence makes sense.

- A shaded space in the chart shows the end of a word.

- Except for the last line, the end of a line is not the end of a word unless there is a shaded space there.

- When you have filled in the chart, answer the question asked.

PROBLEM

299.

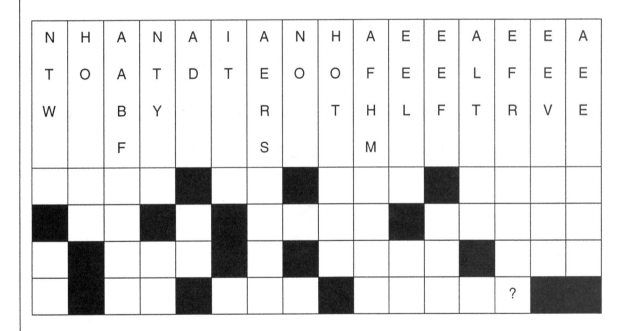

Reference

*Algebra
Word
Problems—
Diophan-
tine
Problems*

*Classroom
Quickies,
Books 1–
3*

DIOPHANTINE PROBLEMS

PROBLEM

300. Morton and Angelica decided that they had bought too much at the garage sales they attended.

Besides that, they had other items they wanted to dispose of, so they decided to hold a garage sale of their own.

They divided their merchandise into four categories:

transportation (bicycle, surfboard, scooter, toboggan, skateboard, wagon, roller skates, ice skates),

clothes,

toys, and

miscellaneous.

They priced the categories at, respectively, 2 for $25, $3 each; $2 each; and 3 for $1.

List the different ways someone can buy 100 items for $100.

(Hint: This is a harder problem that the others about Morton and Angelica. There are ten ways to be listed.)

Reference

Classroom Quickies, Books 1– 3

WEIGHING BALLS

PROBLEM

301. You have four each of golf balls and table-tennis balls.

With the exception of one ball in the eight, all balls of one kind weigh the same.

The odd ball looks just like the others of its kind. You know that its weight is different from the others but not whether it is heavier or lighter.

You have a balance scale. Find the odd ball in no more than three weighings.

Teaching Suggestions and Answers

Introduction
Many people assume that the critical thinking needed for mathematics automatically transfers to other subject areas. Research, however, shows that no such transfer generally occurs *unless the student is taught to think critically in a variety of contexts.*

It has also been shown that not only is there no transfer of critical thinking activity outside the subject area but that there is often no transfer *even within the subject area* unless the teacher *teaches for transfer.*

The remedy for this is to involve the student in many facets of critical thinking, both inside and outside a mathematical context, so that (s)he is likely to think critically when confronted with new information.

Consequently, many of the problems in this series do not involve mathematics per se but concentrate rather on developing various aspects of critical thinking needed for success in mathematics. These aspects include the following:

- analyzing a problem to determine a solution (rather than jumping to a conclusion)
- applying old knowledge to new situations
- arriving at a conclusion by process of elimination
- catching contradictions and inconsistencies
- deductive reasoning
- determining whether information is relevant or irrelevant
- distinguishing among possible, probable, and necessary inferences
- inductive reasoning
- learning that there may be various ways to solve a problem
- looking for a logical starting point in a problem that seems unsolvable
- organizing data so that it can be more easily used
- perceiving logical patterns
- using proof by contradiction (indirect proof)
- realizing that a problem may have more than one acceptable solution
- reasoning by analogy
- trying something to see if it works when logic doesn't suggest a solution

- weighing given information to determine truth or falsity

General Information
In some subjects, learning need not occur in a particular order. In geography, for example, knowledge about the frequency of earthquakes and other natural phenomena in country X can come before or after knowledge of X's rivers and principal industries, which, in turn, can come before or after any knowledge about country Y.

In arithmetic, however, we have a different situation. Long division comes after subtraction and multiplication, which, in turn, come after addition; division by a two-digit number comes after division by a one-digit number. Nearly every new arithmetic process learned needs application of a previous process learned thereby demanding a review of, and broadening the scope of, prior knowledge.

In recognition of the merit of review, much of the new material introduced at one level in this series is reintroduced at a higher level. With rare exceptions, however, the difficulty of the problems increases as the level increases. The exceptions occur for one of three reasons: (1) The problem has proved to be fun for various ages; (2) A relatively difficult problem is included at a lower level so that the gifted student is challenged; or (3) A relatively easy problem is included at a higher level so that the slower student has success.

Students tend to react negatively to a crowded textbook page and to give it only cursory attention in order to get through it. The result, of course, is that not much critical thinking occurs. On the other hand, the students are suspicious of a comparatively empty page and tend to concentrate on and think about the material there because they intuitively feel that it can't be as easy as it looks.

With this in mind, nearly every page in this series has a generous amount of white space, and the amount of white space on any one page is pretty much in direct proportion to the amount of thought or discussion required to solve the problems on it. In fact, sometimes only one relatively short problem appears on a page, and in these cases intuition is correct: the problem, which may or may not *look* simple, either requires a good deal of thought or has a history of needing much class discussion because different students produce different answers for it.

A few routine problems are included in some sections of this series in order to give the students practice in using a new concept, but the great majority of the problems are designed to stimulate critical thinking. Most of the pages are intended to be used as supplementary materials taking fifteen minutes or so of class time.

Problems range from relatively easy to relatively hard. To judge whether or not you think the problem is appropriate for your class, it is suggested that you do each problem yourself before assigning it.

At the bottoms of some pages are either statements or questions that have no bearing on the other material there. Some are included simply because they are interesting to think about or to know, and others are intended either as nonsense or as mild jokes.

Several of the problems in this series are similar to problems that can be found in recreational mathematics books. Such books usually have a different Dewey decimal number (793) than ordinary books on mathematics (510), but recreational problems can sometimes be found in both of these categories, as well as others. Check with your school and public librarians for their practices in numbering such books.

ARITHMETIC LEVELS OF THIS SERIES

Not all schools are able to teach an optimal arithmetic curriculum. High absenteeism, lack of parental support, and negative peer pressure can combine to frustrate the teachers' attempts to stick to the syllabus. With this in mind, the arithmetic required by the problems in this series has been geared toward the reduced syllabi.

This does not imply that the critical thinking levels of the problems have also been limited. The ages of the intended students have been considered, but otherwise it has been assumed that whatever arithmetic the students know, they are capable of thinking critically about it.

Specifically, the ages and arithmetic knowledge assumed are as follows:

BOOK 1: 8–10 years old, grades 3–4. The arithmetic assumes only the most basic knowledge of fractions (such as knowing that half of twelve is six) and includes no complicated addition or subtraction, no long multiplication or division, and no

decimals, percents, or areas. Multiplication is usually limited to knowing simple facts such as $3 \times 4 = 12$. Division is similarly restricted.

BOOK 2: 10–12 years old, grades 5–6. It is assumed that the student can handle integral addition and subtraction, simple long division and multiplication, addition and subtraction of simple mixed numbers, and multiplication and division of simple fractions. With one exception, no three-digit divisors are used. No complicated fractions, percents, or areas are included. Problems involving decimals are limited to students who use hand calculators. These same problems offer alternative numbers to students who must figure by hand.

BOOK 3: 12–14 years old, grades 7–8. Reasonable facility with the four basic operations using integers or fractions is expected. Decimals rarely appear and then are limited to simple percent or money problems or to students who use hand calculators. A working knowledge (but not a profound understanding) of percents and simple areas is assumed. Some problems involve simple powers.

BOOK 4: age 14 years and older, grades 9–12. The arithmetic here expects general facility with the four basic operations on integers, fractions, and decimals, along with the ability to work reasonably well with percents and areas. Some problems involve simple powers and simple square roots. No college preparatory mathematics knowledge is expected, but some problems demand fairly complex reasoning about arithmetic.

REFERENCES

At the top left of many pages you will see the word "REFERENCE" followed by one or more titles. These titles correspond to the list below and indicate that similar material can be found in these Critical Thinking Books & Software publications.

ALGEBRA WORD PROBLEMS
    AGES AND COINS
    DIOPHANTINE PROBLEMS
    FORMULAS, RECTANGLES, D=rt
    FUN TIME
    HOW TO SOLVE ALGEBRA WORD PROBLEMS
    MISCELLANEOUS A-1
    MISCELLANEOUS B-1
    MISCELLANEOUS C-1
    MIXTURES
    PERCENTS AND WORK RATES
    TEACHER'S MANUAL AND DETAILED SOLUTIONS
    WARM-UP

BASIC THINKING SKILLS

CLASSROOM QUICKIES
    BOOK 1
    BOOK 2
    BOOK 3

CRITICAL THINKING, BOOK 1

CRITICAL THINKING, BOOK 2

CROSSNUMBER™ PUZZLES
    SUMS: BOOK A-1
    SUMS: BOOK B-1
    SUMS: BOOK C-1

DEDUCTIVE THINKING SKILLS (MIND BENDERS®)
    MIND BENDERS®—A1
    MIND BENDERS®—A2
    MIND BENDERS®—A3
    MIND BENDERS®—A4
    MIND BENDERS®—B1
    MIND BENDERS®—B2
    MIND BENDERS®—B3
    MIND BENDERS®—B4
    MIND BENDERS®—C1
    MIND BENDERS®—C2
    MIND BENDERS®—C3
    MIND BENDERS®—INSTRUCTIONS AND
        DETAILED SOLUTIONS
    MIND BENDERS®—WARM-UP

INDUCTIVE THINKING SKILLS

MATH MIND BENDERS®
    BOOK A-1
    BOOK B-1
    BOOK C-1
    WARM UP
    WARM UP-2

MATH WORD PROBLEMS

TEACHING THINKING

If we are to encourage our students to think critically, we have to give them time to do so, for critical thinking entails more than simply looking at a problem and immediately knowing the answer. With this in mind, avoid doing your students' thinking for them. Encourage them to reason out the answers themselves.

Don't think you have to know all the answers. If you're really teaching your students to think critically, they'll ask many questions you won't be able to answer.

Students are proficient imitators. Show by example the way you want them to react under various conditions:

- Encourage questions, including questions about opinions you've expressed.
- Treat the students courteously and insist they be courteous to each other during a discussion. An argument can be spirited, even heated, without resorting to name-calling or other derogatory comments. Don't allow something like, "That's really a stupid thing to say!" to pass. Insist that the student who says it either apologize or back it up.
- Make learning a team effort, with yourself as part of the team.
- Don't try to fake your way. If you change your mind about an answer, tell the students, particularly if it was their arguments that convinced you. If you don't know an answer, say forthrightly, "I don't know." You might like to add something to that admission: "I wonder how we could find out?" Or, "That's beyond my education." Or, "Let me think about it and see if I can come up with an answer for tomorrow."
- Encourage class discussion, especially of different
  - viewpoints
  - ways of looking at a problem
  - ways of attacking a problem
  - answers to a problem

Some problems might be too hard for an individual student to solve and unsuitable for discussion by the full class. Try grouping the students in sets of three to five to work on these. Decide on the groupings beforehand so that you have at least one good thinker, and preferably two, in each group. Avoid grouping the best and poorest thinkers together. Have the students move their desks so that each group is a self-contained circle.

ANSWERS AND COMMENTS

Pages 1–2

ANSWERS

1. If the first native told the truth, then the second native lied. If the first native lied, then the second native told the truth. Either way, one of them told the truth and the other lied, so the third native had to be lying.

2. a–b. Whether or not the first native is a liar, he would claim that he is not a liar. Then the first part of the second native's statement brands

the second native as a liar, and the second part of his statement (since we now know he was lying) makes the first native a truth-teller.

3. a–b. Following the same reasoning as in problem 2, the first part of the second native's statement tells us that the second native is a liar, and the second part of his statement tells us that the first native is also a liar.

Pages 3–6

How often have we seen outlandish answers to mathematical problems? For example, a student gets an answer of 45 to the problem 45×9 because "Everyone knows that 0 is nothing, so 45 is the same as 405." (Yet the same student will readily agree that $405 is not at all the same as $45.) Or a student adds three numbers, each of which is between 10 and 20, and is not at all disturbed when his or her answer is not between 30 and 60. It sometimes seems as though such students suspect that mathematics has something to do with magic, in which case, they reason, one answer should be as good as another.

There are various degrees of likelihood to be considered when choosing whether or not to accept something. Among these are fact, highly probable, more likely than not, fifty-fifty, possible but not probable, possible but unlikely, and impossible. Wishful thinking and fantasy probably come somewhere between the last two.

It is important that students learn to think about given information and to distinguish among the various degrees of likelihood. As a first step toward this goal, the two problems following are designed to press the student to make relatively easy decisions about likelihood. Each case is a matter of deciding simply whether a story falls within the bounds of reasonable possibility or whether it falls so far outside these bounds that it becomes mere wishful thinking or fantasy.

ANSWERS
  4. a. True to life
     b. Fantasy
     c. True to life
  5. a. True to life
     b. True to life
     c. Fantasy
     d. Fantasy
     e. True to life
     f. Fantasy

g. Fantasy. (It is important that the students acknowledge the fantasy in this story, for it appears to summarize the wishful thinking of some of them. It is true that an arithmetic lesson may be understood when a previous one was not, but in such a case one of two things will be true, both of which were denied in the story: either the new lesson will clear up the confusion about the previous lesson, or the new lesson will not be based on knowledge taught by the previous lesson.)

Page 7
ANSWERS
  6. in front of Royal Crescent
  7. 72
  8. Yes

Pages 8–9
On page 8, the students should deduce from the last example (no bulldog is green) and from the last paragraph that a statement might be proved false in several ways, of which finding a counterexample is just one. (Working on the principle that there will be at least one student who hasn't made the inference, however, you'd better mention it to the class.)

ANSWERS
  9. a. No. This has no bearing on the statement.
     b. No, but I'm open to argument, assuming that Marty is a teenager. This says Marty *can't* have a pet, not that he *shouldn't*.
     c. No. No example is given.
     d. No. No example is given.
     e. Yes, assuming that Sam is a teenager.
     f. No. This argues that she shouldn't have a dog or a cat as a pet, but what about a canary or a parakeet or a gerbil or a turtle or a couple of goldfish?
     g. Yes

Pages 10–1
ANSWERS
  10. a. Yes
      b. Yes
      c. No
      d. Yes
      e. No
      f. No

g. Yes
h. No

Pages 12–4
ANSWERS

11. No. This kind of statement cannot have a counterexample.

12. a. Yes. This does not support the statement.
    b. No. This supports the statement.
    c. No. This doesn't say in what respect Revere supported Washington. Perhaps he supported him as a general against English troops but not as a presidential candidate. Even if the statement implies support for Washington's candidacy as president, it does not imply that Revere expected Washington to win.

13. a. No. The objection may be true, but it doesn't give an example to prove the statement false.
    b. Yes. Whether or not the rating was accurate, Aunt Miriam is obviously a great chef.
    c. No, but it might come close. The compliments could reflect friendship and appreciation of the effort behind good cooking rather than an ability to distinguish between great cooking and excellent cooking.

14. a. No. The statement talks only about girls.
    b. No. The statement talks only about teen-aged girls.

15. a. No. This doesn't disagree with the statement.
    b. No. He may like adventure stories, too.
    c. No. No example is given.
    d. No. This supports the statement.

16. No. This kind of statement cannot have a counterexample.

Pages 15–6

Although the general rule in this textbook is to include only as much on one page as the students should be expected to learn or solve in one session, these two pages of problems do not follow that rule. There are several items on each page. It would probably be a good idea to expect a saturation point to be reached before a page is completed. Plan to end the session at that point and then come back to the remaining items another day.

ANSWERS

17. No. A counterexample is an example that proves a (general) statement to be false, so there can be no counterexample to a true statement.

18. For this problem, encourage the students to think of a set of two statements to use as a model. That is, the two given statements are in the form, "All [word or phrase #1] are [word or phrase #2]. I found a [#1] that is not a [#2]." The questions become less abstract if the students substitute meaningful words or phrases for #1 and #2. Their first statement should be true for some, but not all, cases.
    a. Yes
    b. Yes
    c. No. All zoffers except the one you found may be middigs.
    d. Yes
    e. Same as (c).
    f. Yes
    g. No
    h. No
    i. No. You've proved that a zoffer doesn't have to be a middig, but not the converse. For example, put zoffers = numbers that can be written as fractions, and put middigs = numbers that can be written as whole numbers. Then the statement reads, "All numbers that can be written as fractions are numbers that can be written as whole numbers." The statement can be disproved by producing the fraction 2/3, but that doesn't prove that some whole numbers cannot be written as fractions.

19. For this problem, too, encourage the students to think of a set of statements to use as a model. It will be helpful if the statement is itself true but has a false converse.
    a. No. Consider the statement "All squares are four-sided figures." Finding a 3 × 5 rectangle is not a counterexample to the statement.
    b. No
    c. No
    d. No
    e. No
    f. No

g. No
h. No
i. No
j. Yes

Pages 17–21

These problems teach the students that the easiest place to start on a problem is not necessarily at the first number one encounters. These problems also teach that one may have to consider and discard various choices before finding one that satisfies all conditions.

Although it may look as though there could be more than one answer, these problems are created so that the answers are unique.

ANSWERS

20.

21.

22.

Pages 22–6

Students too often make unwarranted assumptions about what they're reading or being told. A painless way to show them that they do this is to supply them with a short story and some conclusions about a subject that is simple to understand, emotionally neutral, and interesting enough to argue about.

Fairy tales and nursery rhymes not only meet these criteria but have the added advantage of being so familiar that the students are doubly likely to allow past impressions of the story to influence their interpretations of what they are now reading.

Use class discussion to decide on the answers. For each answer, ask first, "How many chose 'true'? How many 'false'? How many 'can't tell'?" and write the numbers on the chalkboard. Ask, "Who wants to start? Tell us which answer you chose and why you think it's right." Try to keep out of the discussion yourself. Let the students argue about it until they are all convinced of the same answer. It will take longer to settle without your intervention, but it will be more effective in developing the students' abilities to think critically.

Don't take for granted that my answers have to be right. I once used the same problem for three different classes, went to the first class *knowing* my answer was right, changed my mind because of the students' arguments, and changed my mind twice more because of the arguments of the students in the other two classes.

Don't think your students are too old for nursery

rhymes and fairy tales. My students were tenth- through twelfth-graders whose abilities ranged from gifted to educable mentally retarded and whose social inclinations ranged from aggressive gang members to shy loners. Despite the ages of the students and the numerous classes exposed to such materials, there were only a handful of times when a student objected to the first problem with a disparaging, "Hey, we're a little old for this kind of stuff, aren't we?" In each case, I said to the class after obviously considering the student's comment, "You could be right at that. I'll tell you what. I'll make a deal with you. If you'll all read the story to your-selves and decide on the first five answers without talking to anyone about them, and if we all agree on the answers, we won't do any more of the problem, and we'll move on to something else." The students thought this fair enough and set to work. It some-times took two class periods (55 minutes each) to agree on the first answer, and that was the end of any objections.

ANSWERS

23. a. ?
    b. ?
    c. ?. I still smile at the argument one of my students gave beamingly years ago to convince me of his "?" answer: "Maybe it's talking about a season. You know—maybe Humpty had a rotten spring, and he had an okay summer, but he had an absolutely great fall!" After the class had groaned at his sense of humor, we conceded he was right.
    d. ?
    e. T. I'm open to argument on this one, but I don't see the point of saying that the king's horses and men couldn't put him or her together again if (s)he wasn't injured.
    f. ?
    g. ?. We're told that they couldn't do it, but maybe this was obvious without their trying.
    h. ?
    i. ?. This one is probably true, as I was in-formed by one of my students some years ago. The class had agreed that it was stupid to include anything to the effect that horses couldn't put Humpty together again, and the next day the student said she'd been curi-ous about why something like that would be included in the first place, so she'd gone to the library to see what she could find out .

She reported that in the old days a king's army had two kinds of fighters—the king's men, who were foot soldiers, and the king's horses, who were soldiers mounted on horses and were considered to be superior to the foot soldiers.

24. a. ?. We don't know whether Jack was little, or whether he was six feet tall and was called "Little Jack Horner" to distinguish him from Big Jack Horner, who is seven feet tall.
    b. T. He "sat in a corner eating." The use of the present participle of the verb "eat" means he was doing both at the same time.
    c. ? Maybe it was a mince pie and a plum fell in by mistake.
    d. ?
    e–f. ?. He said he was, but maybe he's a liar.
    g. ?. A Christmas pie may be a pie baked for Christmas, or it may be a pie (mince, for example) often served at Christmas time but also served at other times.

25. a. ?
    b. F
    c. T
    d. ?
    e. T
    f. F
    g. ?
    h. ?
    i. F
    j. T
    k. T
    l. F. From the given information, Anton is two years older than Gerda. If he is also twice as old as Gerda, then he is four and Gerda is two. But if he is four, he cannot be five years older than Marthese. This contradicts what we are given. Therefore, Anton cannot be twice as old as Gerda.
    m. T

Pages 27–50, 152–5

One of the most important mathematical tools is the ability to recognize and use analogies. When we show our students how to solve a few problems, we want them to apply analogous reasoning to other problems. When we introduce new material, we want them to recognize the similarities and respect the differences between these new ideas and what they already know.

Analogues abound in mathematics. For example, multiplication and addition are analogous, as are division and subtraction. Telling the time seventeen hours after twelve o'clock (using a twelve-hour clock) is analogous to finding the least residue of 17 (mod 12). Arithmetic operations in base ten are analogous to those in base sixteen. A problem asking how many nickels are in $5.25 is analogous to one asking how much would have to be invested at 5% in order to earn $5.25 in interest. Problems involving percents are readily translatable to problems involving fractions or decimals. And if you'll excuse the pun, the reasoning needed to prove plane geometry theorems often runs parallel to that needed for proving theorems in analytic geometry.

If we are to have students who easily recognize analogous situations in mathematics, it is necessary that they learn to look for similarities and differences, that they learn that order matters, that they learn to distinguish between situations that are close enough to be analogous and situations that are not, and that they have practice in forming analogies.

This could be accomplished utilizing only mathematical notions, but it is much easier for the students to learn when the practice exercises use everyday words not taken exclusively from any one subject area. (Presenting an assortment of topics also has the advantage of showing that analogies can be applied in numerous contexts.) Consequently, most of the material on the next several pages has little to do with mathematics per se, but it has a great deal to do with building knowledge necessary to success in mathematics.

After the word *analogous* is introduced in the textbook, it will be assumed throughout the rest of the book that the students will understand an instruction such as, "Use analogous reasoning to show...."

Pages 27–8
ANSWERS
26. finished
27. sighted
28. vista
29. snowball
30. rebuke
31. cut out
32. receptor
33. count

Page 29
Encourage alternate answers to these problems. We want the students to learn to notice various similarities among apparently different things, for such discernment is a prerequisite to the successful use of analogical reasoning in mathematics.
ANSWERS
34. infrequent
35. answers to arithmetic operations
36. lack of interest
37. leaders
38. recipe instructions
39. dimensions

Page 30
Other answers are not only possible but likely. Encourage class discussion of answers.
ANSWERS
40. large residences; penthouse
41. nonroutine; interesting
42. talking softly; moan
43. talking loudly; howl
44. results of immoderate anger; anger
45. change; correct

Pages 31–2
ANSWERS
Other answers are possible.
46. tortoise
47. mammoth
48. 8/12
49. 2 yards
50. question
51. contradict
52. negative
53. lively

Pages 33–4
ANSWERS
54. more, less
55. gentleman, lady
56. precede, succeed
57. false teeth, eyeglasses
58. friend, ally
59. mutton, beef
60. quart, gallon
61. conjecture, given

Pages 35–7

ANSWERS

62. increase, decrease / product, quotient / part, whole / take away, add to / quotient, sum
63. start, end / contract, shrink / assist, interfere / veteran, beginner / reserved, exuberant

Pages 38–9

Many standardized tests measure knowledge by including analogies among the test questions. However, a wrong answer there may not indicate lack of knowledge about the subject matter. Instead, it may show confusion about what is being asked. This is because in everyday life we don't necessarily compare or contrast two pairs of things by using the standard analogical words "is to" and "as." These words don't make a lot of sense in such a context unless we think about them and figure out how they're being used, or we've seen them used previously in such a way and now understand how they relate the terms to each other.

As you discuss this section with your class, keep in mind that an analogy using "is to" and "and" will not, to many of the students, immediately make sense. To help them understand, choose a simple analogy and try stating it in various ways.

Ignoring whether or not good English is used, or even whether or not the statements are entirely accurate, here are some examples of other ways to state the analogy, "Up is to down as high is to low":

- Up and down are related in the same way that high and low are related.
- Up is related to down the way high is related to low.
- Up and down contrast in the way that high and low contrast.
- Up is different from down in the way that high is different from low.
- The relation between up and down is like the relation between high and low.

Similar examples can be formulated using such terms as these: dissimilar, opposite, opposed (to), reversed (from), and contrary (to).

So that the students don't get the idea that the first two terms of an analogy must name opposites, you will probably want to show that analogies can be formed for other relationships, too. At the same time you give a nonstandard form, be sure also to state the standard form. Note the following examples:

- A cow and its calf are related in the way that a mare and its foal are related. (A cow is to its calf as a mare is to its foal.)
- Laugh and happy sound go together just like cry and sad sound go together. (Laugh is to happy sound as cry is to sad sound.)
- Green light means "go" just as red light means "stop." (Green light is to "go" as red light is to "stop.")
- Penthouse apartment is related to plenty of money in the same way that tenement flat is related to lack of money. (Penthouse apartment is to plenty of money as tenement flat is to lack of money.)

Stress two things: (1) an analogy must always make good sense; (2) an analogy cannot necessarily be formed from two pairs of terms even if the terms of one pair are related not only to each other but to the terms of the other pair. For example, a hammer and a wrench are both tools, and both are owned by humans; a dog and a cat are both pets, and both are owned by humans. Despite these similarities, however, it wouldn't make good sense to say any of these (or any of the 20 other statements that could be made from arranging the four terms in different orders):

> Hammer is to wrench as dog is to cat.
> Hammer is to wrench as cat is to dog.
> Hammer is to dog as wrench is to cat.
> Hammer is to cat as wrench is to dog.

Ask the students to think of analogies themselves (using "is to" and "as"), and let the class discuss whether or not the analogies created are good ones. This not only will supply examples on the students' level but will also lessen confusion about the meaning of an analogy stated in standard form.

ANSWERS

64. Elephant is to ant as large is to small. (For the student who chooses "strong, weak," you might like to point out that an ant is extraordinarily strong for its size.)
65. Elephant is to ant as herd is to colony.
66. Linger is to hasten as dawdle is to rush.
67. Repair is to maintain as cure is to prevent.
68. Acute is to obtuse as sharp is to blunt.
69. Hammer is to saw as clobber is to slice.

Pages 40–1

In the "don't be fooled" paragraph on page 40, the second sentence is accurate only if the four given terms are different from each other. If two of the terms are the same, there will be only twelve distinct ways to arrange them, of which just four will be in correct order for forming analogies. For example, given the terms

       ocean, lake, lake, puddle,

they can be arranged as

       ocean, lake, lake, puddle;
       ocean, lake, puddle, lake;
       ocean, puddle, lake, lake;
       lake, ocean, lake, puddle;
       lake, ocean, puddle, lake;
       lake, lake, ocean, puddle;
       lake, lake, puddle, ocean;
       lake, puddle, ocean, lake;
       lake, puddle, lake, ocean;
       puddle, ocean, lake, lake;
       puddle, lake, ocean, lake;
       puddle, lake, lake, ocean.

The only acceptable analogies would be

       ocean is to lake as lake is to puddle,
       lake is to ocean as puddle is to lake,
       lake is to puddle as ocean is to lake,
       and puddle is to lake as lake is to ocean.

ANSWERS

To avoid having to list eight answers for each problem, a general solution is given here, and then only a first answer is given for each problem. General rule:

	term	is to	term	as	term	is to	term
If	first		second		third		fourth
then	first		third		second		fourth
and	second		first		fourth		third
and	second		fourth		first		third
and	third		first		fourth		second
and	third		fourth		first		second
and	fourth		second		third		first
and	fourth		third		second		first

70.	bird	nest	lion	lair
71.	Canada	China	N.A.	Asia
72.	merchant	sell	customer	buy
73.	attorney	dentist	client	patient
74.	tennis	bowl	court	alley

Pages 42–6

These problems will be too obscure for some of the students to figure out by themselves, and yet to invite a full class discussion could easily lead to so many suggestions and comments that confusion, rather than solution, results. Instead, break up the class into several small groups, say three to five students each, and let each group work independently on solving the problem.

Pages 42–5
ANSWERS

75. metal = <u>nickel</u>
football period = <u>quarter</u>
male deer = buck = <u>one dollar</u>
worth of (fish structure) = worth of (fin) = worth of $5-bill = <u>five dollars</u>
Result: Nickel is to quarter as one dollar is to five dollars.

76. aparsonc = in ac parson = in ac curate = <u>inaccurate</u>
edeedx = in ex deed = in ex act = <u>inexact</u>
$\frac{\text{nose}}{\text{the}}$ = <u>on the nose</u> = <u>accurate</u>
discarded stage routine = ex-act = <u>exact</u>
Result: Inaccurate is to inexact as on the nose is to exact, or inaccurate is to inexact as accurate is to exact.

77. (amusement park ride that's thrilling) but (with no hair curler) = (roller coaster) (with no roller) = <u>coaster</u>
(dwow) (pain) = (w in dow) pane = window pane = <u>glass</u>
(put) (tahhsittocS) = place (backward Scottish hat) = place (backward tam) = <u>place mat</u>
recordless tr = record less tr = platter – tr = <u>plate</u>
Result: Coaster is to glass as place mat is to plate.

78. confused blot = <u>bolt</u>
(timepiece) that was (sightless) at first but not later = (clock) that was (no-see) at first but not later = clock without first c = <u>lock</u>
(bowling target) follows [(vault) before (beverage)] = pin follows (safe before tea) = pin follows safety = <u>safety pin</u>
(strikes) [(out-of-order) an object] in (fascinating her) = deletes [(out-of-order) a thing] in fascinating her = deletes atingh from fascinatingher = fasciner = <u>fastener</u>
Result: Bolt is to lock as safety pin is to fastener.

Page 46

In the hint given the students, the words *puzzling*,

crafty, *open*, and *obvious* are approximate synonyms for *elusive*, *subtle*, *candid*, and *apparent*, the terms of the analogy.

ANSWER

79. (bus coming from the opposite direction) leads [(unique) (unseeing) (floor lids)] = sub leads [(singular) (without eyes) (floor covers)] = sub leads [singular (without i's) (tiles)] = sub leads [singular (without i's tiles)] = sub leads (singular tles) = sub leads tle = <u>subtle</u>

   e untied if = e loose if = <u>elusive</u>

   (able able) (10 10 do) = (able two) (past 10s do) = (able to) (past tense do) = (can)(did) = <u>candid</u>

   1 having a (young to-do) = one having a (young stir) = one having a youngster = a parent = <u>apparent</u>

   Result: Subtle is to elusive as candid is to apparent.

Pages 47–50

We are reasoning by analogy any time we use a previous experience to predict the outcome of a new experience. For example, "That plant had green leaves and I was told to pull it out because it was a weed. This plant has green leaves, so it must be a weed, too." Or, "I got yelled at yesterday because I was running in the school hallway. If I run in the school hallway today, I'll get yelled at today, too."

Make sure the students understand that when reasoning by analogy assumes a cause-and-effect relationship, it is the quality of the relationship that determines whether or not the analogy is a good one. In the first example above, the speaker assumes that having green leaves causes a plant to be classified as a weed. Since having green leaves has no bearing on whether or not a plant is called a weed, the analogy is a poor one. In the second example above, it is assumed that running in the school hallway causes the runner to be reprimanded. On the surface, this assumption is false, and yet the analogy is a good one because running in the hallway can be dangerous and it is this potential danger, rather than the running itself, that results in the reprimand.

The students will automatically look for similarities between analogous situations, but you may have to lead them to evaluate the relative importance of the points of agreement.

All analogous situations have differences, too, and some students are likely to say that a particular analogy is poor because differences outnumber similarities. Consequently, you may have to stress to the students that when they are deciding on the quality of an analogy, they are to distinguish between important and unimportant differences.

Here are some other examples of reasoning by analogy.

• That steel bar is metal, and my fingernail doesn't make a dent in it. Since this aluminum foil is also metal, my fingernail won't make a dent in it, either. (Poor.)

• My house is at sea level, and I got scalded when some boiling water splashed on my wrist. I'm now near a campfire on top of a mountain 15,000 feet high, and my wrist will get scalded if boiling water splashes on it. (Poor, since water boils at a much lower temperature at high altitudes outdoors.)

• My friend went to a beauty parlor for a facial, and when they were done she didn't have any wrinkles. So if I go to that beauty parlor and have the same operator give me a facial, then I won't have any wrinkles. (Not enough information. How old is my friend? How old am I? Did my friend have any wrinkles before the treatment? Do I have any wrinkles?)

• Three different batteries for my toy lasted only a month each. So if I get another of the same kind of battery and use the toy the same amount of time, the new battery will last only a month. (Good.)

Use class discussion for these problems. We want the students to be exposed to the reasoning of their classmates and to hear the arguments they use.

ANSWER

80. Make sure the students realize that Jaime's analogy is, "I'm trying to learn a computer programming language this semester, and I don't understand it. Therefore, if I try to learn another computer programming language later on, I won't understand it, either." Jaime also seems to be assuming that he will still not understand the present language if he repeats the class in a year or two.

   For two main reasons, this is a poor analogy:(1) The successful use of a computer programming language requires a certain standard of logic, and the logic of an eighth grader is seldom as developed as it will be when that person is in the tenth or eleventh grade. Therefore, the fact that Jaime now has trouble learning a language does not imply that he would have trouble learning it a couple of years from now. (2) Computer programming languages vary in difficulty. For example, assembler language is much harder to learn than BASIC. It follows that Jaime may not have much trouble learning the other language even though he is having trouble learning this one. Of course there may also be other factors to account for Jaime's difficulty with this class: Maybe the textbook is unclear. Maybe the teacher's explanations are unclear. Maybe Jaime has been given extra responsibilities at home and is too tired to give the class the attention it needs. Maybe Jaime doesn't realize that the computer is brainless, that it doesn't know what to do when it encounters a mis-spelled word or an extra comma.

Pages 49–50

ANSWERS

81. Poor. The fact that different things were wrong today than yesterday and that Nigel discovered his mistakes shows that he understands what was to be done. The cookies turn out well when his mother makes them, so the recipe is not at fault. Nigel appears to think that the cookies have turned out badly because of some unforeseeable factor when in reality his own carelessness was the cause both times.

82. Judging only on the basis of what we've been told, this is a poor analogy, for the only similar-ity we see between the two cases is that both people are females.

Pages 51–61

Many of us are used to calling a mathematical function, say addition, an "operation," and this terminology is correct. However, a function is an operator as well as an operation. The symbol used to denote the function, say +, is also an operator.

As a point of interest, computer programming manuals consistently refer to mathematical func-tions as "operators" rather than "operations," and their symbols used as operators include not only +, –, * (multiplication), and / (division), but grouping characters such as ( ) and (( )), logical operators such as "not", "and", and "or", and conditional operators such as < and <=.

Rather than call, say addition, an operation and

call its symbol, +, an operator, it is consistent with modern usage and less confusing to the students to say "operator" for both the operation and its symbol.

The order of precedence stated in the textbook is followed both in mathematics and in computer programming.

The operators ( ), [ ], $\times$, $\div$, /, +, and –, as well as exponentiation (raising to a power), are discussed. More operators are discussed in CRANIUM CRACKERS BOOK 4. For both books, the computa-tions involved, while sometimes complex, do not result in large numbers and so do not require the use of a hand calculator.

For the grouping symbols ( ) and [ ], you will notice, in the textbook examples as well as in the answers in this manual, that the outer symbols are not "reduced" when the inner symbols have been eliminated. For example, the solution of
$$24 - [18/(4 + 5) + 10] = ?$$
is shown as
$$24 - [18/(4 + 5) + 10] = 24 - [18/9 + 10] =$$
$$24 - [2 + 10] = 24 - 12 = 12.$$

Some current mathematics textbooks are following computer programming practice by using only ( ). In that case, the problem shown here would be written as
$$24 - (18/(4 + 5) + 10).$$

I'm likely to write the problem that way when work-ing on my own, but the students generally find it confusing. As a result, both ( ) and [ ] are used in this textbook. Although a common practice is to change the [ ] to ( ) once the original ( ) have been eliminated, this, too, results in confusing some students. Furthermore, I don't see any purpose in doing it. Consequently, the grouping symbols that the problem starts with are the symbols that are used throughout the solution.

It is assumed that the students know what it meant by an expression such as 2^3.

Pages 54–5

Stress the importance of working from left to right. Although it doesn't matter for addition and multipli-cation because they are associative, subtraction and division are not associative, and most students won't stop and think about this if they feel like starting at some point other than the left end. For example, $24/4/2 = (24/4)/2 \neq 24/(4/2)$, and $10 - 5 - 4 = (10 - 5) - 4 \neq 10 - (5 - 4)$.

Insist that the students show their work so that you can verify their reasoning.

ANSWERS

Answers will vary.

83. $4 - 3 - 1 = 1 - 1 = 0$
84. $4 - 1 \times 3 = 4 - 3 = 1$
85. $4 - 3 + 1 = 1 + 1 = 2$
86. $1^3 + 4 = 1 + 4 = 5$
87. $4 + 3 - 1 = 7 - 1 = 6$
88. $4 + 1 \times 3 = 4 + 3 = 7$
89. $1 + 3 + 4 = 4 + 4 = 8$
90. $4 \times 3 - 1 = 12 - 1 = 11$

Page 56–7

You will want to be able to follow the students' reasoning, so make sure they show their work. In actual practice, we don't usually show as much detail as is shown in the lesson examples and in the answers below. Instead, we do all equivalent operations at the same time. For instance, the first answer below would be more likely to look like this:
$21/(5 - 2) + (6 + 2) \times 2 = 21/3 + 8 \times 2 = 7 + 16 = 23$.
The detail is shown, however, so that there is no question about the order in which the computations are to be done.

ANSWERS

91. $21/(5 - 2) + (6 + 2) \times 2 = 21/3 + (6 + 2) \times 2 =$
$21/3 + 8 \times 2 = 7 + 8 \times 2 = 7 + 16 = 23$
92. $48 - [2 \times (1 + 4) + 8 \times 4] = 48 - [2 \times 5 + 8 \times 4] =$
$48 - [10 + 8 \times 4] = 48 - [10 + 32] = 48 - 42 = 6$
93. $27/3^2 \times 8 = 27/9 \times 8 = 3 \times 8 = 24$
94. $24/(2^3 + 2^2) + 15 - 3 = 24/(8 + 2^2) + 15 - 3 =$
$24/(8 + 4) + 15 - 3 = 24/12 + 15 - 3 =$
$2 + 15 - 3 = 17 - 3 = 14$
95. $2 \times 3^2 - [35 - 4 \times (2 + 5)] =$
$2 \times 3^2 - [35 - 4 \times 7] =$
$2 \times 3^2 - [35 - 28] = 2 \times 3^2 - 7 =$
$2 \times 9 - 7 = 18 - 7 = 11$
96. $(3 + 2) \times (7 - 4) - (6 \times 4 - 7 \times 2) =$
$5 \times (7 - 4) - (6 \times 4 - 7 \times 2) =$
$5 \times 3 - (6 \times 4 - 7 \times 2) = 5 \times 3 - (24 - 7 \times 2) =$
$5 \times 3 - (24 - 14) = 5 \times 3 - 10 = 15 - 10 = 5$
97. $7 \times 8 - 2 \times 10 - [4 \times (7 - 4) \times 2 + 5] =$
$7 \times 8 - 2 \times 10 - [4 \times 3 \times 2 + 5] =$
$7 \times 8 - 2 \times 10 - [12 \times 2 + 5] =$
$7 \times 8 - 2 \times 10 - [24 + 5] = 7 \times 8 - 2 \times 10 - 29 =$
$56 - 2 \times 10 - 29 = 56 - 20 - 29 = 36 - 29 = 7$
98. $24/6/2 + (3 + 4) \times 11 - (5 + 8 \times 9) =$
$24/6/2 + 7 \times 11 - (5 + 8 \times 9) =$
$24/6/2 + 7 \times 11 - (5 + 72) =$

$24/6/2 + 7 \times 11 - 77 = 4/2 + 7 \times 11 - 77 =$
$2 + 7 \times 11 - 77 = 2 + 77 - 77 = 79 - 77 = 2$
99. $21 + 9 - [3 \times (1 + 5) - 36/4] =$
$21 + 9 - [3 \times 6 - 36/4] = 21 + 9 - [18 - 36/4] =$
$21 + 9 - [18 - 9] = 21 + 9 - 9 = 30 - 9 = 21$
100. $(4 + 3) \times (7 - 4) - [6 \times (7 - 4) - 2^3] =$
$7 \times (7 - 4) - [6 \times (7 - 4) - 2^3] =$
$7 \times 3 - [6 \times (7 - 4) - 2^3] = 7 \times 3 - [6 \times 3 - 2^3] =$
$7 \times 3 - [6 \times 3 - 8] = 7 \times 3 - [18 - 8] =$
$7 \times 3 - 10 = 21 - 10 = 11$
101. $2 \times (6^2 \div 3/2 + 25 - 4 \times 7) =$
$2 \times (36 \div 3/2 + 25 - 4 \times 7) =$
$2 \times (12/2 + 25 - 4 \times 7) = 2 \times (6 + 25 - 4 \times 7) =$
$2 \times (6 + 25 - 28) = 2 \times (31 - 28) = 2 \times 3 = 6$

Pages 58–9

Make sure the students show their work step by step, as in the answers below.

ANSWERS

102. $(12 - 3) \times (2 + 9) = 9 \times (2 + 9) = 9 \times 11 = 99$
103. $22 - (3 \times 2 + 9) = 22 - (6 + 9) = 22 - 15 = 7$
104. $12 - [4 \times 5 - 2 \times (6 + 1)] = 12 - [4 \times 5 - 2 \times 7] =$
$12 - [20 - 2 \times 7] = 12 - [20 - 14] = 12 - 6 = 6$
105. $4 \times (1 + 6) - (9 \times 3 - 6) = 4 \times 7 - (9 \times 3 - 6) =$
$4 \times 7 - (27 - 6) = 4 \times 7 - 21 = 28 - 21 = 7$
106. $(5 + 13) \div (6 - 4) \times 4 = 18 \div (6 - 4) \times 4 =$
$18 \div 2 \times 4 = 9 \times 4 = 36$
107. $(6 + 2) \times 9 - (13 - 7) \times 7 = 8 \times 9 - (13 - 7) \times 7 =$
$8 \times 9 - 6 \times 7 = 72 - 6 \times 7 = 72 - 42 = 30$
108. $6 \times 9 - 3 \times (7 + 1) - 21 = 6 \times 9 - 3 \times 8 - 21 =$
$54 - 3 \times 8 - 21 = 54 - 24 - 21 = 30 - 21 = 9$
109. $8 \times (10 - 36 \div 9) + 2 - 2 \times 5 \times 5 =$
$8 \times (10 - 4) + 2 - 2 \times 5 \times 5 =$
$8 \times 6 + 2 - 2 \times 5 \times 5 = 48 + 2 - 2 \times 5 \times 5 =$
$48 + 2 - 10 \times 5 = 48 + 2 - 50 = 50 - 50 = 0$
110. $(3^2 + 1) \times 5 - (2 + 4) \times 8 =$
$(9 + 1) \times 5 - (2 + 4) \times 8 = 10 \times 5 - (2 + 4) \times 8 =$
$10 \times 5 - 6 \times 8 = 50 - 6 \times 8 = 50 - 48 = 2$
111. $[4 \times (10 - 7) - 2] \times 2^3 - 1 = [4 \times 3 - 2] \times 2^3 - 1 =$
$[12 - 2] \times 2^3 - 1 = 10 \times 2^3 - 1 = 10 \times 8 - 1 =$
$80 - 1 = 79$
112. $[3^2 + 2^3 - 24 \div (6 - 4)] \times (18 \div 9)^2 =$
$[3^2 + 2^3 - 24 \div 2] \times (18 \div 9)^2 =$
$[3^2 + 2^3 - 24 \div 2] \times 2^2 = [9 + 2^3 - 24 \div 2] \times 2^2 =$
$[9 + 8 - 24 \div 2] \times 2^2 = [9 + 8 - 12] \times 2^2 =$
$[17 - 12] \times 2^2 = 5 \times 2^2 = 5 \times 4 = 20$

Pages 60–1

These problems provide an admirable way to meet several teaching goals:

- Students do drill work but feel as though they're taking a break.
- The problems are open-ended in two ways: first, there is no guarantee of a solution for any given problem; second, there may be many solutions to a given problem.
- The problems require creative thinking, for there are numerous possible combinations that can be tried (most of which won't work) in order to get an answer.
- The problems demand critical thinking because each time a combination is tried, it must be analyzed and either accepted or rejected. If it is rejected, the student then must try to figure out what is wrong with it and what needs to be changed in order to make the result acceptable.
- The problems provide a gentle way for the students to learn that (1) not all arithmetic problems have solutions, and (2) for some problems that have solutions, these solutions may have to be found by trial and error and process of elimination.
- Even though finding a particular answer may take several minutes, the students do not react to their temporary lack of success with a loss of self-confidence, for they understand what is to be done, and they know how to go about doing it.
- The problems present an agreeable challenge. Students enjoy trying to find answers and are likely to spend some of their free time trying to do the problems.

  If your students like competition, you could issue a challenge to see who can come up with the greatest number of correct answers for a given problem. For example, $6 = (3 \times 4) \div (1 \times 2) = (4 \times 3) \div (1 \times 2) = \ldots = 1 + 3 + 4 - 2 = 3 + 1 + 4 - 2 = \ldots = 12/4 + 3 =$ other combinations, too. Or the challenge could be to see who can find solutions for the longest list of numbers. If you decide on this one, it would probably be a good idea to set an upper limit, say 50 or 100. Otherwise, you're likely to be faced with computations such as 32×41 and 34^{12}.

Some of the more inventive students may come up with solutions such as $1 = 1^{234}$ and $6 = 4^{1/2} \times 3$

ANSWERS

113. There are many ways to get answers. A quick run-through found solutions for all but five of the whole numbers from 0 through 100. I did not find solutions for 53, 74, 89, 95, or 99. Of the ninety-six solutions found, seven used one or both of decimals and square roots, and two used summation signs (Σ). There may, of course, be simpler solutions for those I solved, as well as solutions for the five problems I didn't solve.

114. As in problem 113, there are many correct answers. A quick run-through for this current set found solutions for all whole numbers from 0 through 100. No summation signs (Σ) were used this time. It was not necessary to use either decimals or square roots for the first fifty problems, but I used one or both of these in at least twenty-five of the last fifty-one problems. There may, of course, be simpler solutions for several of the problems in the last half.

Pages 62–5

ANSWERS

115.

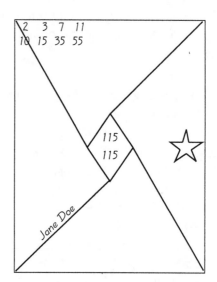

116. Yes. Maybe Irwin is the teacher.

117. Yes. Limetown and Appleton could be on opposite sides of Big City.

118. No. If they did, then Oakton and Elmtown would either be on the same side or on opposite sides of Big City, and in neither case do the distances tally.

119. 5071. (She doesn't count the first 64 numbers. $5135 - 64 = 5071$.)

120. (6×20) minutes + (5×20) seconds = 120 minutes + 100 seconds = 121 minutes 40 seconds = 121 2/3 minutes = 2 hours 1 2/3 minutes

121. none

122. 33
123. none

> The term was coined in about 1599. First question: I'm not sure, but I think it was to avoid being accused of robbery by inadvertently counting out less than 12. Penalties for robbery were harsh (including chopping off a hand), and a baker, a member of the "lower orders," didn't stand much chance against an accusation by a member of the aristocracy. Second and third questions: I don't know.

Page 66

Puzzles like this provide excellent opportunities for the students to exercise their critical thinking abilities. There are several discoveries for them to make, among which are:

1) When only one letter appears, it can be filled in.
2) When a word contains only one letter, that letter is *A* or *I*.(A single letter could also be an initial—e.g., Robert E. Lee—but not in these particular puzzles.)
3) To make the remaining choices more obvious, used letters should be crossed off.
4) Only certain letters can be used to begin or end a two-letter word. For example, no two-letter word begins with *C* or *R*, so if the letters *C*, *R*, and *T* are in a column where a two-letter word begins, then *T* is the choice to make. The only ordinary two-letter words starting with *T* are *TO* and *TV*, so any other letters appearing in the next column can usually be ruled out.
5) A three-letter word starting with *TH* is *THE* or *THY*.
6) A three-letter word starting with *Y* is probably *YES*, *YET*, or *YOU*. A three-letter word ending with *U* is probably *YOU*.
7) A four-letter word starting with *TH* is probably *THAT*, *THAN*, *THEM*, *THEN*, or *THEY*.
8) Only certain sequences of letters are probable. For example, words don't begin or end with *RW* or *PM* (but they might begin with *WR* or end with *MP*).

ANSWER

124. How much is a dozen dozens divided by half a dozen dozens? [(12 × 12) ÷ (6 × 12) = 2]

Page 67

This is a typical Diophantine problem. If we try to solve this problem by straight algebra, we'll have three variables but only two equations—a setup that has an infinite number of solutions. However, a Diophantine problem has built-in conditions that limit the number of solutions. For example, Angelica and Morton can't buy a fraction of a jacket or a negative number of books.

The mathematics needed for a *formal* solution of a Diophantine problem is beyond the knowledge of a general mathematics student, but such students nevertheless enjoy trying to solve the problems.

A side benefit of presenting the students with Diophantine problems is that the students learn that not all problems are as straightforward as they sound and that such problems can be solved by trial and error.

There are three more Diophantine problems in this textbook.

For information about how to solve Diophantine problems (which may be helpful to you but not to your general math students), as well as for more Diophantine problems to give your students, see the booklet *Diophantine Problems* in the ALGEBRA WORD PROBLEMS series.

ANSWER

125. They bought 80 books, 16 pairs of jeans, and 4 jackets.

Page 68

ANSWER

126. Fill the 9-quart jug and use it to fill the 3- and 5-quart jugs. Discard the water in the 3-quart jug. This leaves 5 quarts in the 5-quart jug and 1 quart in the 9-quart jug, a total of 6 quarts.

> He knew the school was a high school.

Pages 69–72

Make sure the students understand these simple ideas. We're going to expand them into adding and subtracting in number bases other than base ten.

ANSWERS

127. 2 o'clock
128. 8 o'clock
129. 6 o'clock
130. 6 o'clock
131. 3 o'clock
132. 5 o'clock
133. 7 o'clock
134. 5 o'clock
135. 6 o'clock

136. 4 o'clock
137. 5 o'clock
138. 2 o'clock
139. 1 o'clock
140. 5 o'clock
141. 3 o'clock
142. 2 o'clock
143. 7 o'clock
144. 2 o'clock

Page 73

Make sure the students understand exactly how Mario does the problems. His method is much easier than counting out the hours one by one on the fingers. Also, it will help avoid mistakes because some students, when asked for the time 5 hours after 10 o'clock (on a 12-hour clock), will start with 10 and count 10 (one), 11 (two), 12 (three), 1 (four), 2 (five), getting an answer of 2 o'clock.

Left to devise their own arithmetic notation for, say a 12-hour clock, the students are likely to write something like "9 + 7 = 16 − 12 = 4." Do not allow such an incorrect use of =. Offer an acceptable alternative such as

$$9 + 7 = 16; 16 − 12 = 4.$$

If your students can work with negative numbers, lead them to discover that negative numbers can be used to solve some clock arithmetic problems. For instance, consider Mario's second example:

"Or say it's 1 o'clock and I want 3 hours ago. If I take 1 − 3, I'll get less than 1, so I add 6 first. I take 1 + 6 − 3 and get 4, so the answer is 4 o'clock."
When Mario found 1 − 3 < 1, he stopped long enough to add 6 to the 1 so that he would get a positive result. If he knew how to use negative numbers, he could get 1 − 3 = -2, which isn't on the clock face, and then add 6 to get his answer of 4. This method computes 1 − 3 + 6 instead of 1 + 6 − 3.

While that example doesn't show much difference in effort expended, the use of negative numbers can be handy when the students start using a 24-hour clock two pages from now. To find the time 22 hours before 5 p.m., the method shown there has them figuring this way:

5 + 12 = 17; 17 − 22 is negative, so add
24 to 17; 24 + 17 = 41; then 41 − 22 = 19.

We see some good possibilities for computation errors there. Using negative numbers, the figuring would be

5 + 12 = 17; 17 − 22 = -5; -5 + 24 = 19

ANSWERS

145. a. Yes. When going forward, the clock counts 1, 2, ..., 6 and then starts at 1 again, in effect discarding the first 6 numbers, and that's what Mario's method does. When going backward, the clock counts 6, 5, ..., 1, and then starts at 6 again, in effect adding 6 each time the next number would be less than 1. Again, that's what Mario's method does.

b. 1) He would use 9s instead of 6s.
   2) Yes. The principle is the same as explained in (a) above for the 6-hour clock.

c. Same as (b) 2 above.

Page 74

ANSWERS

146. a. Yes. We already know that Mario's method always works. The only difference between his method and Choon-Wei's is that Mario does the problem while working with a large number to be added or subtracted, afterwards reducing the answer by multiples of 6, while Choon-Wei reduces the large numbers to be added or subtracted before doing the problem. The two methods give identical results.

b. She would find 15 − 7 − 7 = 1 and add that to 2, getting an answer of 3 o'clock.

c. Yes. Mario's method works for all clocks and, as explained in (a) above, Choon-Wei's method gives the same results.

Pages 75–6

Encourage the students to try several examples in order to convince themselves that they can use exactly the same computations with this clock that they used for a 6-hour clock whose numbers were 1–6, except that whenever they would have had an answer of 6, they will now have an answer of 0. Make sure they understand that this applies only to a final answer—i.e., that they still have to add or subtract multiples of 6, not 0, when doing their computations. For example, 19 hours after 2 o'clock, it will be 2 + 19 − 6 − 6 − 6 = 3 o'clock.

If your students can work with negative numbers, ask them if they could have a 6-hour clock whose numbers were -1, 0, 1, 2, 3, 4. Let them discuss the idea and try out some problems for it. (The answer is yes. In this case, we would be replacing 5 with -1, and since -1 = 5 – 6, this is a workable idea. Just as intermediate computations were not affected by replacing 6 with 0, so they will not be affected by replacing 5 with -1. For example, to find the time 21 hours after 2 o'clock, we would compute 2 + 21 = 23, 23 – 24 = -1 instead of 2 + 21 = 23, 23 – 18 = 5.)

ANSWERS

147. 2 o'clock
148. 4 o'clock
149. 0 o'clock
150. 5 o'clock
151. 4 o'clock
152. 0 o'clock
153. 2 o'clock

Pages 77–85

ANSWERS

154. 7 p.m.
155. 10 a.m.
156. 1 p.m.
157. 7 p.m.
158. 2 a.m.
159. 4 p.m.
160. 9 a.m.
161. 12 p.m.
162. 1 p.m.
163. This is OK if we keep our heads screwed on straight while we're doing it, but it leaves room for careless mistakes. If we're going to figure answers as suggested, then we have to follow these rules:
1) An answer of 24, or answers from 1 through 11 will be
   a. a.m. if the starting hour was a.m.
   b. p.m. if the starting hour was p.m.
2) Answers from 12 through 23 will be
   a. a.m. if the starting hour was p.m.
   b. p.m. if the starting hour was a.m.
For example, to compute 14 hours after 3 p.m., we would take 3 + 14, get 17, and have to remember that this will designate an a.m. hour in this case since we started with a p.m. hour.
164. 1700
165. 1300
166. 1200
167. 0500
168. 2000
169. 2400
170. 0150
171. If you are a third as old as your uncle Ebenezer,

who is forty-five, how old are you? (15)
172. Fill the 7-gallon jug and empty the contents into the 4-gallon jug, discarding the first 4 gallons. This leaves 3 gallons in the 4-gallon jug. Now fill both the 7-gallon and the 2-gallon jugs.
173. Not enough information is given. Maybe not all water used by the Freeman family is from the water company. For example, maybe they live next to a lake and they pipe lake water up to the house for baths and housecleaning and lawn sprinkling.

Page 86

This is strictly a class discussion problem. If you think, as I did, that this problem's answer is so obvious that your students will be insulted by being given the problem, you have a surprise coming. I've found that the usual answers are gains of 0, $10, $20, or $30, with an occasional answer of a loss of $10, $20, or $30.

Ask the students to call out their answers, and write all the answers on the chalkboard. Then ask, "Who wants to start? Tell us which answer you got, and tell us how you got it." The hard part for the students comes when you say, after hearing the explanation, "We have some other answers here, and we can't have more than one right answer to the problem, so if you think another answer is right, you should be able to tell us what's wrong with the reasoning we've just heard."

The time needed for the discussion usually takes at least a full class period. I've never told my students the answer to the problem. Instead, they have always managed to prove which answer is correct.

ANSWER

174. Not given. Let the students battle it out.

Page 87

Unless they have seen this kind of problem before, some of the students will have no idea of how to go about finding the answers. Aside from suggesting that they sketch a picture, or figure, for each problem, it is recommended that you not tell them how to do these problems. These are good problems for developing critical thinking ability.

ANSWERS

175. a–c. The mat's position doesn't matter. It covers the same number of square feet of floor space no matter where it is. The uncovered floor space is the total area of the floor, 9 ft × 12 ft = 108 sq ft, minus the area covered by the mat, 4 ft × 4 ft = 16 sq ft, or 92 sq ft.

　　d. The mat now covers 2 ft × 2 ft = 4 sq ft less of the floor's area, so the uncovered area is 96 sq ft.

Page 88

ANSWERS

176. a. 117 pounds
　　　b. 32.4 pounds
　　　c. 18 pounds
　　　d. 5.4 pounds
　　　e. 2.7 pounds
　　　f. 1.8 pounds
　　　g. 2.7 pounds

Pages 89–97

Students tend to be confused when, after having been carefully taught to distinguish between numerals and numbers, they read a sentence such as, "What are the factors of 12?" It's obvious to them that 12 is a numeral, and a numeral is just something made from a given set of symbols, so how can a numeral have factors? Or maybe the factors are the symbols that make up the numeral, and so the factors of 12 are 1 and 2?

A different, but related, question is raised in the students' minds when they read, "What are the factors of the number 12?" because now they read that the symbol 12 is no longer a numeral but has suddenly become a number, which they know is not possible. So perhaps the question should be, "What are the factors of the number represented by the numeral 12?" That seems to be a complicated way to ask what should be a simple question.

The textbook avoids such difficulties by saying "number" when referring either to a numeral or to a number. This is correct usage according to the dictionary, and the students are not confused, for they judge by context (as they do for so many other words).

Pages 89–92

The concepts in part I of the lesson are so well known that the students may tend to skim through the material, thinking it too elementary for them. To know something and to understand it thoroughly, however, are two different things, and what we want

is for the students to understand these ideas so well that they will be able to apply analogous reasoning to number bases other than base ten in Part II of the lesson.

The value of our written numbers depends on both the base used and the place a digit occupies. The definition of a "base n number system" includes the stipulation of place value for each digit.

Our way of writing numbers is sometimes called a "base and place number system." Not all number systems use the concept of base and place. For example, Roman numerals (how many digits are there?) do not have a place value; XI = 11, and XC = 90, showing that X takes a value of 10 one time and a value of -10 another time, even though it is in the same place both times.

ANSWERS

177. 1, 2, 3, 4, 10, 11, 12, 13, 14, 20, 21, 22, 23, 24, 30, 31

178. 1, 2, 3, 4, 5, 10, 11, 12, 13, 14, 15, 20, 21, 22, 23, 24, 25, 30, 31

179. 1, 2, 3, 4, 5, 6, 10, 11, 12, 13, 14, 15, 16, 20, 21, 22, 23, 24, 25, 26, 30, 31

180. 1, 2, 3, 4, 5, 6, 7, 10, 11, 12, 13, 14, 15, 16, 17, 20, 21, 22, 23, 24, 25, 26, 27, 30, 31

181. a. The difference would be 8. If we did convert the two numbers to base ten, we'd have 8 × 96 and 8 × 97, a difference of 8. Encourage the students to realize this without actually doing the multiplication and subtraction involved. There are at least three ways they could think of this:

　　1) Regardless of how much 97 × 8 and 96 × 8 are, 97 8s is one more 8 than 96 8s.

　　2) Think of 97 8s as a list of 8s to be added. Think of 96 8s the same way:
　　　97 of these: 8 + 8 + 8 + ... + 8 + 8
　　　96 of these: 8 + 8 + 8 + ... + 8
　　　Now when we subtract one list from the other, all 8s except the last one in the 97 string will be eliminated.

　　3) If your students are familiar with the distributive property, use it here: 8 × 97 − 8 × 96 = 8 × (97 − 96) = 8 × 1 = 8.

　　b. Same answer. The last digit doesn't matter because it is a units digit (i.e., × 1) for all three bases and so will be eliminated when finding the difference between the two numbers.

Page 93

ANSWERS

182. We're going to add and subtract in base eight exactly as we do in base ten, except that we will remember to regroup by eights instead of by tens. For example, here are three base eight problems:

$$\begin{array}{r} 65 \\ +34 \\ \hline 121 \end{array} \qquad \begin{array}{r} 64 \\ -34 \\ \hline 31 \end{array} \qquad \begin{array}{r} 65 \\ -35 \\ \hline 27 \end{array}$$

(The computations in this explanation are in base ten.) For the first problem, $5 + 4 = 9 = 8 + 1$, so we enter 1 and carry an eight to the eights column. Then $1 + 6 + 3 = 10 = 8 + 2$, so we enter 2 and carry an eight × eight to its column. The second problem looks the same in both base ten and base eight. For the third problem, we take an 8 from the eights column, giving us a top number of $8 + 4 = 12$. Then $12 - 5 = 7$. We're left with 5 eights in the eights column, and $5 - 3 = 2$.

The first computation becomes clearer when we remember than $8_{ten} = 10_{eight}$, so $9_{ten} = 11_{eight}$. We enter the second 1 and carry the first 1 to the eights column. Then $10_{ten} = 8_{ten} + 2_{ten} = 10_{eight} + 2_{eight} = 12_{eight}$, so we enter 2 and carry 1 to the eight × eights column.

Pages 94–8

ANSWERS

183. 230
184. 434
185. 2301
186. 21124
187. 103000
188. 113
189. 117
190. 161
191. 658
192. 1112
193. $23_{four} = 11_{ten} = 21_{five}$
194. $221_{three} = 25_{ten} = 41_{six}$
195. $244_{five} = 74_{ten} = 112_{eight}$
196. $317_{eight} = 207_{ten} = 1312_{five}$
197. $127_{nine} = 106_{ten} = 211_{seven}$
198. $345_{six} = 137_{ten} = 162_{nine}$

199. $3123_{four} = 219_{ten} = 1003_{six}$
200. $1001010_{two} = 74_{ten} = 1022_{four}$
201. How much is twelve divided by the quantity of two divided by three? $[12/(2/3) = 12 \times 3/2 = 18]$

Page 99

The problem should involve finding the answer to
$$(21{,}280 \times 3{,}600)/5{,}280$$
This answer on a calculator is 14,509.090909..., so the students using calculators will know that the whole-number part of the answer is 14,509, even though they don't know that the decimal fraction of .090909... is 1/11.

What we want them to do is apply the knowledge that a quotient times a divisor, plus a remainder, equals a dividend. Here, they know everything except the remainder, so if they take the quotient (14,509) times the divisor (5,280), their answer (76,607,520) will be short of the dividend ($21{,}280 \times 3{,}600 = 76{,}608{,}000$) by the amount of the remainder (480). So the fractional part of the answer is 480/5,280, which reduces to 1/11.

The numbers are easier to handle in a case like this if some reducing is done beforehand. For this problem, the prime factors of 5,280 are 2, 2, 2, 2, 2, 3, 5, and 11. All but 11 are also factors of $21{,}280 \times 3{,}600$. This means that the original problem,
$$(21{,}280 \times 3{,}600)/5{,}280,$$
can be reduced to the problem
$$159{,}600/11.$$
When the calculator now shows an answer of 14,509.0909..., it is simple to do the necessary figuring: $14{,}509 \times 11 = 159{,}599$, which is 1 short of 159,600, so the remainder must be 1 and the fraction must be 1/11.

ANSWER

202. 14,509 1/11

Page 100

ANSWER

203. Weigh all six, three per pan. This will show which pan contains the odd ball. Remove all three balls from the other pan. Of the three still in a pan, put one in the other pan and put one aside. If the scale doesn't balance, you'll know which pan holds the odd ball. If the scale does balance, the odd ball is the one put aside.

Pages 101–7

Many students seem to take for granted that almost anything said during a discussion has a bearing on the topic. They assume that if a comment touches on a peripheral issue, then it is germane to the subject at hand. This is evidenced by their thinking, for example, that an assignment to write a theme on "Why I Like Dogs" is satisfied by a theme on "Why I Like Dogs Better Than Cats."

The ability to differentiate between relevant and irrelevant thoughts is vital to critical thinking in mathematics. When we are doing a three-column addition problem, for instance, it doesn't do much good to think about how multiplication of fractions is done, but it does help to think about how a two-column addition problem is done and to apply the same principles here.

Use class discussion for these problems. Although the directions don't ask for reasons for the answers, ask the students why they chose their answers. Their reasons will help clarify the difference between relevant and irrelevant comments both for themselves and their classmates.

Pages 101–7

ANSWERS

204. a. No
b. No
c. Yes
d. Yes
e. Yes
f. Yes, if they intend to put this idea to Louis. No, if it's simply a comment about Louis's jokes.
g. No. This discusses a way to get Louis to stop pulling practical jokes but not a way to make him realize that some of his practical jokes are dangerous.
h. No

205. a. Yes
b. Yes
c. No
d. No
e. No
f. Yes
g. Yes
h. No
i. Yes
j. No

206. a. No

b. No
c. Yes
d. No
e. Yes
f. No
g. No
h. No
i. Yes
j. Yes

Pages 108–10

Finding patterns is an important aspect of mathematical development. Most answers will probably agree with the simple patterns shown in the answers below. However, students are used to having only one correct solution to a problem and may assume that an answer must be wrong if it doesn't agree with everyone else's answer, so do encourage those who found different patterns to tell the others about them. This will not only reassure such students but will also demonstrate to the rest of the class that there can, indeed, be more than one logical answer to some kinds of problems.

Also, there can be more than one correct explanation for a given answer, and the students should be asked for their lines of reasoning. For example, when I wrote problem 4, I was thinking of the pattern described in the answer below, but it would be more obvious to think of the pattern as "list the counting numbers, and insert between them the even numbers starting with 4," or as "add 3, subtract 2, add 4, subtract 3, add 5, subtract 4, and so on."

ANSWERS

207. 15, 19, 21, 25 (Pattern: add 2, add 4.)
208. 22, 88, 86, 344 (Pattern: multiply by 4, subtract 2.)
209. 15, 30, 31, 62 (Pattern: double, add 1)
210. 10, 5, 12, 6 (Pattern: add 3, divide by 2, add 4, divide by 2, add 5, divide by 2, and so on.)
211. 20, 26, 33, 41 (Pattern: add 1, add 2, add 3, and so on.)
212. 81
213. 123456789101112
214. 224 (Pattern: double)
215. 1432
216. 1314 (Pattern: skip every 3rd numeral)
217. 7/8
218. 8/81 (Multiply by 2/3.)

Pages 111–3

Stress to the students that a light-year is a measure of distance, not a measure of time. Once they have grasped this concept, questions about time (e.g., "How long does it take for light to reach Earth from Proxima Centauri?") may confuse them, and it may take several examples of analogous problems to clarify the situation.

Suggested examples are as follows:

- You want to go 100 miles (distance). How long will it take (time) if you go at 50 mph (rate)?
- A racehorse ran at an average speed of 30 mph (rate). How long did it take (time) for the horse to go around a 1-mile track (distance)?
- Your friend's house is 264 feet away (distance). If you run all the way at 15 mph (rate), how many seconds (time) will it take you to get there?
- The sun is 93,000,000 miles away (distance). Light travels at 186,000 miles a second (rate). How long does it take the sun's light to reach us?
- Proxima Centauri is 4.3 light-years away (distance). Light travels at 186,282 miles a second (rate). How long does it take light from Proxima Centauri to reach Earth?

Encourage the students to use hand calculators for these problems. They will have to use their critical thinking abilities to figure out how to get the calculator to do the required work when the numbers to be entered or the answers are beyond the calculator's capacity. (If the problem requires division, and if the divisor has more digits—not counting trailing zeros—than the calculator's capacity, allow the divisor to be rounded off.)

ANSWERS

219. a. calculator, $186,281.7 \times 1.609344 =$
    $299,791.3362048$
    hand, $186,000 \times 1.6 = 297,600$
  b. calculator, $299,791.3$
    hand, $300,000$

Note for answers 220–224: First answers are for 186,000 and 365; second answers are for 186,281.7 and 365.25.

220. a. 3,600
  b. 86,400
  c. 31,536,000; 31,557,600

221. a. 669,600,000 miles; 670,614,120 miles
  b. 16,070,400,000 miles; 16,094,738,880 miles
  c. 5,865,696,000,000 miles;
    5,878,603,375,920 miles

222. 5,865,696,000,000 miles; 5,878,603,375,920 miles

223. For the computation by hand, there are $24 \times 365 = 8,760$ hours in a year, so the space ship would travel 8,760,000,000 miles in that time. Then the answer is $5,865,696,000,000 \div 8,760,000,000 = 669\ 3/5$ years. For the calculator users, the space ship would travel $1,000,000 \times 24 \times 365.25 = 8,766,000,000$ miles in a year, so one light year would take $5,878,603,375,920 \div 8,766,000,000 = 670.61412$ years $\approx 670\ 3/5$ years.

224. a. 25,222,492,800,000; 25,277,994,516,456
  b. 4.3 years

Pages 114–22

ANSWERS

225. First answers are for 186,000; second answers are for 186,281.7.
  a. 8 minutes 11 seconds; 8 minutes 11 seconds
  b. 8 minutes 28 seconds; 8 minutes 27 seconds
  c. 8 minutes 20 seconds; 8 minutes 19 seconds.

226. $239,000 \div 186,000$ and $238,857 \div 186,281.7$ both give an answer of something over 1.28 seconds, so the answer to the problem is $1\frac{1}{4}$ seconds.

227. a. 143,077 miles a second
  b. 124,000 miles a second
  c. 77,500 miles a second

228. If you start with five dollars and spend a dollar and forty-three cents, how much do you have left? ($3.57)

229.

> Jane Doe
>
> c. IAMGOODLOOKINGBUT
> d. IAMGOODLEEKINGBUT
> e. IAMGOODLEEKINGBUTIA
> f. IAMGOTODLETEKINGBUTITA
> g. IAMGOTODLETEKINGABUTIT
> h. IAMNOTODNETEKIGABUTIT
> i. IAMNOTODNEITEKGABUTIT
> j. IAMNOTCODNCEITEKGABUTIT
> k. IAMNOTCONCEITEDABUTIT
> l. IAMNOTCONCEITEDABOUTIT

230. Laurence, Gerald, Wilma, Toby

231. hamburger, $1.69 a pound; bread, 79¢ a loaf; onion, 39¢

232. not enough information

233. $14.40

234. 18 hours

235. Multiplication and division are both distributive over addition, so we can treat the original number chosen and the 4 that was added to it as two separate problems with respect to these two operations. It will also be noticed as we go along that the instructions to "subtract 18" and "subtract 10" can be applied entirely to the 4 that was added and was then increased by the other operations. Here are the results of following the instructions:

Choose a number	n	
Add 4	n	4
Multiply by 6	$6n$	24
Subtract 18	$6n$	6
Divide by 3	$2n$	2
Multiply by 5	$10n$	10
Subtract 10	$10n$	0
Divide by 10	n	0

As we see, the end result is simply the number we chose.

(I don't know.)

236. a. Three. When the first pawn is chosen, the color doesn't matter. If the second pawn's color matches it, we're done. If it doesn't, then the third pawn's color has to be the same as one of the first two.

b. Nine. The first eight chosen may all be the same color.

237. 10 weeks. This is a matter of finding the least common multiple (LCM) of 5 days and 2 weeks, or 5 days and 14 days. Since the LCM is 70 days, it will be 10 weeks.

((S)he likes red better than blue.)

Pages 123–8

These grids work like crossword puzzle grids, except that digits, rather than letters, are written in the squares.

The first three problems are simply to give the students the experience of using the grid correctly. The other problems are fun to solve and teach the students that the logical place to start a solution is not necessarily at the first clue one encounters.

They also teach that one may have to consider and discard various choices before finding one that satisfies all conditions.

ANSWERS

238. Four answers are possible because 1-A and 1-D can be exchanged, as can 4-D and 5-A.

239. Two answers are possible because 1-A and 1-D can be exchanged.

240. This is not possible. There are only four two-digit answers, and two of these (4-D and 5-A) must end with the same digit.

Pages 127–8

Encourage the use of hand calculators for these problems.

ANSWERS

241. Jane's (9-A) and Carla's (11-D) ages are one-digit numbers, while Ann's age has two digits (2-A). 3-D forces the last digit of Ann's age to be 1, so the three ages are, respectively, 8, 6, and 11. This forces 3-D, 6-A, 1-D, and 1-A. From 4-A, we know that 8-D ends in 5 (not 0 since 10-A can't start with 0), so 10-A is 56. This forces 7-A, 8-D, and 4-A, and fills in all squares.

242. Use Kerry's formula to find 1-D, 9591. From this, answers are forced for 10-A, 3-D, 7-A, 2-A, and 4-A, which fills in all squares.

1 9		2 5	3 2
4 5	5 6		6 3
7 9	3	8 1	
9 1		10 2	11 4

Page 129

This is another Diophantine problem.

ANSWER

243. Of pairs of socks, T-shirts, and blouses, they will buy, respectively, 68, 31, 1; or 72, 24, 4; or 76, 17, 7; or 80, 10, 10; or 84, 3, 13.

(S)he'd heard it called a chest of drawers.

Pages 130–2

ANSWERS

244. Fill the 7-liter jug. Use it to fill the 3-liter jug twice, pouring both 3-liter quantities into the 10-liter jug (to conserve water). Pour the remaining liter of water (from the 7-liter jug) into the 3-liter jug. Now fill the 10-liter jug and use it to fill the 3-liter jug. This leaves 8 liters of water in the 10-liter jug. Discard the water in the 3-liter jug and fill this jug again from the 10-liter jug. Discard this, too. There are 5 liters left in the 10-liter jug.

245. The result of adding or subtracting any number of even numbers is always an even number. No. The arithmetic involved prohibits getting an odd number for an answer regardless of what we choose to call the answer.

246. a. $30; $10

b. 1/2

c. 1 1/2 or 1.5 or 3/2

Page 133

The thing to realize about this problem is that each typist works for eight minutes to type one page.

ANSWERS

247. a. 8

b. 8

c. 32

Pages 134–47

ANSWERS

248. 9615 + 958 = 10573

249. $17.50

250. a. 231 a year

b. Chickens × egg production per chicken per day × days ÷ 3 eggs per omelet = omelets, so 25,000,000 × 1/2 × 6 ÷ 3 = 25,000,000. I don't know what color the majority of the chickens are, but I thought it was an interesting question. (*Are* some colors of chickens better egg-layers than others?)

251. How much is two and a half percent of two dollars and eighty cents? (7¢)

252. Since both people used the same seven letters, we can ignore the point values of all letters except *C* and *H*. Gregory's total was 2 × 4 points + 3 × 2 points = 14 points, while Leila's total was 2 × 2 points + 3 × 4 points = 16 points, so Leila's word was worth 2 points more than Gregory's.

(seven)

253. Parenthesized numbers refer to clue numbers in the problem.

The buffalo has a yellow collar (1). The red collar is not worn by the vulture (5) or the zebra (6), so the cheetah wears it.

The vulture isn't the pet of Allan (5), Daphne (4), or Eunice (3), so it is Howard's pet. Its collar isn't green (2), so it is white. Then the zebra's collar is green. The cheetah isn't Allan's (5, red collar) or Daphne's (4), so it is Eunice's. Eunice isn't Franklin (3), Jackson (6), or Kingsley (4, cheetah), so she is Lohmer. Howard, who has the vulture, isn't Franklin (3) or Kingsley (4), so he is Jackson. Daphne isn't Kingsley (4), so Allan is, and Daphne is Franklin.

Franklin's pet is not the zebra (3, green collar), so it is the buffalo, and so Kingsley has the zebra.

Allan Kingsley, zebra, green
Daphne Franklin, buffalo, yellow
Eunice Lohmer, cheetah, red
Howard Jackson, vulture, white

254. Parenthesized numbers refer to clue numbers in the problem.

Jeannine likes all the drinks (4), so she isn't Hopper (1), Gardner (2), or Casey (8). Also, she isn't Martin (6), so Jeannine is Kulper. Since Martin doesn't get along well with the person whose favorite drink is lemonade (5), but Martin is a good friend of Jeannine (6), Jeannine's favorite drink is not lemonade. It is not iced tea or orange juice (4) or apple juice either (6), so it is pineapple juice.

The orange juice drinker, who gets along with everyone (3), isn't Bernard (7) or Edwin (5) or Dorothy (3), so she is Faith.

Martin doesn't get along well with the lemonade drinker (5), but the orange juice drinker gets along well with everyone (3), so Martin doesn't drink orange juice. Martin doesn't drink lemonade (5) or apple juice (6), so (s)he drinks iced tea. The lemonade drinker is not Casey (5) or Gardner (2), so (s)he is Hooper.

Martin gets along well with at least two people (6) but Bernard doesn't (7), so Martin is not Bernard. Martin isn't Faith (orange juice) or Edwin (5), so Martin is Dorothy. Casey is female (8), so she is Faith.

Edwin is not the lemonade drinker (5), so he isn't Hooper. Then Bernard is Hooper, and Edwin is Gardner and drinks apple juice.

Bernard Hooper, lemonade
Dorothy Martin, iced tea
Edwin Gardner, apple juice
Faith Casey, orange juice
Jeannine Kulper, pineapple juice

255. Yes

256. chicken, turkey, pork, beef, veal

257. Yes. Psychiatrists (at least in Michigan) are required to be medical doctors.

258. a. 5/6
b. 2/5
c. 3/5
d. 3 3/4
e. 1 7/8
f. 1 1/4
g. 3

259. The statement has to be true for any population of at least 200,002. The first 200,001 people may all have different numbers of hairs (ranging from 0 through 200,000). If they don't, then we already have the required pair, but if they do, then the 200,002nd person has a number of hairs between 0 and 200,000, inclusive, and so must have the same number of hairs as someone else. (Note: My reference books didn't tell me the maximum number of hairs that can grow on a human head, so I pulled a figure out of the air.)

I don't know.

260. There will be over 3 feet of space between the belt and the ground now, so that's enough for most people to walk under if they stoop over and keep their knees bent.

There are three things to realize here. First, the belt, which was 25,000 miles long, is now 25,000 miles + 20 feet long, so the circumference of the circle made by the belt has been increased by 20 feet. Second, $C = \pi d$, so $d = C/\pi$. Third, if the sum of two numbers is divided by a third number, the answer is the same as if the two numbers were each divided by the third and then the answers were added. For example, $(12 + 18)/2 = 30/2 = 15$, and $12/2 + 18/2 = 6 + 9 = 15$.

This means that whatever the circle's original diameter was—i.e., (25,000 miles)/π—the diameter has increased by (20 feet)/π, which is just over 6 1/3 feet. This is an increase of about 3 1/6 feet, or 3 feet 2 inches, in the radius, and that's how much space is now between the belt and the ground.

261. 53¢

The S was only an initial. Harry Truman's full name was Harry S. Truman. His parents chose the middle initial so that both of his grandfathers, Solomon Young and Anderson Shippe Truman, could claim that he was named for them.

262. Maybe Norman's school is much smaller than Catherine's so that meals cannot be prepared as economically. Maybe Norman's cafeteria serves more expensive foods than Catherine's—e.g., salmon, steak, asparagus, ice cream as opposed to tuna, pasta, beets, sherbert. Maybe Norman's school is private and Catherine's is public so that Catherine's school gets government aid and Norman's school doesn't. Maybe Norman goes to a private elementary school and Catherine goes to a public high school.

Simpson, in a way. Ulysses S. Grant's name was Hiram Ulysses Grant. His parents always called him by his middle name, and the congressman who appointed him to the U.S. Military Academy thought "Ulysses" was his first name and that his middle name was his mother's family name, Simpson. Consequently, the congressman made out the appointment to Ulysses S. Grant. Grant, who thought that his real initials, H.U.G., would expose him to teasing from his classmates, didn't bother correcting the name.

Page 148

This is another Diophantine problem.

ANSWER

263. They can buy 1 set of tires, 3 computer games, 6 shirts, and 90 miscellaneous items, or 2 computer games, 18 shirts, and 80 miscellaneous items.

Pages 149–51

ANSWERS

264. No

265. Yes

266. Yes. They could live in different time zones.

267. a. 10

   b. 9

(Benjamin Franklin)

268. Fill the 7-liter jug from the spring and use this to fill the 5-liter jug. Empty the 5-liter jug and dump the remaining 2 liters from the 7-liter jug into it. Fill the 7-liter jug from the spring again, and use this to fill the 5-liter jug. This leaves 4 liters in the 7-liter jug. Empty the 5-liter jug, and dump the remaining 4 liters from the 7-liter jug into it. Fill the 7-liter jug from the spring again, and use this to fill the 5-liter jug. This leaves 6 liters in the 7-liter jug. Empty the 5-liter jug.

(I don't know.)

Pages 152–75

The students may not realize at first that they have worked with proportions many times before, and it would be helpful to remind them that every time they have added or subtracted fractions with unlike denominators they have written at least one proportion. For example, given the fractions 2/3 and 5/6 to add, they have written "2/3 = 4/6" and probably also "5/6 = 5/6."

It is important that the students have clear ideas about the parts of a proportion, their relation to each other, the significance of the equal sign, and the difference between a ratio and a proportion.

The equal symbol denotes a symmetric relation, so this is always true:

If item 1 = item 2, then item 2 = item 1.

All fractions are ratios. Although there are various kinds of ratios, all ratios in this book are fractions, so for the most part the two words can be used synonymously by the students.

There is a difference in the thinking involved about the two concepts; however, a fraction, say 3/4, is thought of as 3 parts out of every 4 parts (of something), whereas the ratio 3/4 is thought of as 3 to 4 because a ratio compares the two things.

For example, in a household comprised of a baby, two parents, and a grandparent, 3 out of 4, or 3/4, of the people are adults, and the ratio of adults to total people is 3 to 4, or 3/4.

A ratio has two terms: $\dfrac{\text{first term}}{\text{second term}}$, or $\dfrac{\text{numerator}}{\text{denominator}}$.

A proportion has two sides, left-hand side = right-hand side, or first ratio = second ratio, and four terms:

$$\frac{\text{first term}}{\text{second term}} = \frac{\text{third term}}{\text{fourth term}}.$$

A proportion is read as "first term is to second term as third term is to fourth term."

As defined here, a proportion consists of two ratios separated by an equal sign, so for our purposes neither of the following is a proportion:

- 4/2 = 2 (but 4/2 = 2/1 is a proportion)
- 4/2 = 24/3 – 6 (but 4/2 = [24 – 18]/3 is a proportion, as is 4/2 = 24/[3 + 9])

In common usage, the terms *ratio* and *proportion* are sometimes used interchangeably. In mathematics, however, the two terms are *never* synonymous. Here are some of the differences:

- A proportion is a statement of equality; a ratio is not.
- A proportion contains an equal sign; a ratio does not.
- A ratio gives the relative sizes of two things; a proportion is a statement that two *pairs* of things have the same relative sizes.
- A ratio is not in itself a statement; a proportion is.
- A proportion has four terms; a ratio has only two.
- A proportion is an equation; a ratio is not.

Page 153

It is not suggested that you raise the matter your-self, but some of the students may conjecture, since any proportion can be written as an analogy, that any numeric analogy can be written as a proportion. If they do bring it up, encourage them to explore the idea. They should be able to think of various coun-terexamples to the conjecture. For instance, if we're talking about differences between numbers, then

1 is to 2 as 5 is to 6, but 1/2 ≠ 5/6.

Or if we're talking about multiplying a number by itself, then

9 is to 3 as 25 is to 5, but 9/3 ≠ 25/5.

In each of these cases, however, no pair of num-bers was a ratio, for a ratio, by definition, is a frac-tion—i.e., an indicated *quotient* of two numbers—and this should be made clear to the students. In the first case above, for instance, to talk about the *difference* between 1 and 2 and then to write "1/2" is contradictory. Although nonproportional numeric analogies can be formed, nonproportional numeric analogies cannot be formed when the numbers compared are ratios.

Pages 154–5

ANSWERS

All the proportions are listed here, although the students are required to state only three of them. However, only the first of the analogies is shown here. In particular, notice that we consider the proportion a/b = c/d to be distinct from the propor-tion c/d = a/b, even though they are equivalent statements.

269. Yes. 1/4 = 2/8; 1 is to 4 as 2 is to 8; 1/2 = 4/8; 2/4 = 1/8; 2/8 = 1/4; 4/1 = 8/2; 4/8 = 1/2; 8/4 = 2/1; 8/2 = 4/1.

270. Yes. 4/1 = 12/3; 4 is to 1 as 12 is to 3; 4/12 = 1/3; 1/4 = 3/12.

271. No

272. Yes. 9/2 = 18/4; 9 is to 2 as 18 is to 4; 9/18 = 2/4; 2/9 = 4/18; 2/4 = 9/18; 18/9 = 4/2; 18/4 = 9/2; 4/2 = 18/9; 4/18 = 2/9.

273. Yes. 3/4 = 12/16; 3 is to 4 as 12 is to 16; 3/12 = 4/16; 16/4 = 12/3; 16/12 = 4/3; 4/3 = 16/12; 4/16 = 3/12; 12/3 = 16/4; 12/16 = 3/4.

274. Yes. 6/15 = 10/25; 6 is to 15 as 10 is to 25; 6/10 = 15/25; 15/6 = 25/10; 15/25 =6/10; 10/25 = 6/15; 10/6 = 25/15; 25/10 = 15/6; 25/15 = 10/6.

275. Yes. 5/10 = 12/24; 5 is to 10 as 12 is to 24; 5/12 = 10/24; 10/5 = 24/12; 10/24 = 5/12; 12/24 = 5/10; 12/5 = 24/10; 24/12 = 10/5; 24/10 = 12/5.

276. No

Pages 156–75

The problems are arranged in their approximate order of difficulty, and problems already done can be used for reference in a current proof. When a problem is easier than a preceding one, it is prob-ably because the easier problem uses as part of its proof the statement proved by the harder problem.

Although they look innocuous enough, these problems require critical thinking and will result in a decidedly improved understanding of ratios and proportions.

Keep in mind that to find the answer to such a problem is one thing, but to prove it, particularly without the help of algebra, is considerably more difficult.

The students may need frequent reminders to choose numbers of their own so that they can see how a problem works. Encourage them to start each problem with easy numbers. For example, if a problem says that two terms of the proportion are the same, they could start with 1/2 = 2/4 or 2/4 = 4/8; or if the terms are all distinct, they could start with 1/2 = 3/6 or 2/4 = 3/6. Once they see how the problem works for these numbers, they can try to generalize their findings so that specific numbers don't have to be used. This generalization is, of course, the hard part of the problem and requires a different level of critical thinking (and a different side of the brain) than merely understanding the problem and trying it out with specific numbers.

Use class discussion to help the students gradu-ate from an intuitive understanding of an idea to the formulation of a proof that their intuition is correct. It will be helpful if you will

- remind them that if both numerator and denomi-nator of a fraction are multiplied or divided by the same (nonzero) number, the fraction's value doesn't change. (Mention again that they've done such multiplication and division when adding or subtracting fractions with unlike denominators.)
- remind them that dividing a fraction by a number is the same as multiplying the fraction by the number's reciprocal.
- teach them that both sides of an equation can be

multiplied or divided by the same (nonzero) number, and the result will also be an equation.
- Show them several examples and assign a few problems for practice, possibly along these lines:
  1) Change each fraction into a fraction having a denominator of 12: 1/2, 2/3, 5/6
  2) Find a common denominator for each pair of fractions, and express both as fractions having that denominator: 2/3, 3/4; 1/2, 3/7; 2/5, 3/20
  (Notice that the least common denominator [LCD] is not asked for. Encourage the students to realize that a pair of fractions can have an infinite number of common denominators.)
  3) Find the LCD for each pair of fractions, and express both as fractions having that denominator: 6/12, 6/8; 6/16, 2/4; 8/24, 4/6
  4) Reduce each fraction as far as possible: 4/6, 10/20, 15/25
  5) Multiply both terms by 2, 3, and 5: 1/2, 3/5, 2/6
  6) Multiply both sides by 3: 1/2 = 3/6; 8/5 = 16/10
  7) Divide both sides by 2: 2/1 = 6/3; 8/9 = 24/27

Even when they can prove something *orally*, you should not expect students at this level to be able to prove it in *writing*, at least not with a conventional proof. Instead, you might like to suggest that they use diagrams (with numbered or lettered parts, if they wish) and arrows to go along with a written explanation.

You will notice that on some pages of the textbook a list of selected problems proved so far is included. This helps the students remember some properties of proportions and serves as a handy reference if needed for the current problem. It is also a sneaky way to let the students know that not everything included on a page is needed for the problem they're doing.

Pages 157–8
ANSWERS

277. The remaining number must be the same as the other three. Two of the three equal numbers must be in one of the ratios, so that ratio is worth 1. Then the other ratio, too, must be worth 1 (in order to have a proportion), and so its two terms must be equal.

278. The sides of an equality can always be switched. (By definition, the equal relation is symmetric.)

279. Examples will vary.
  a. 1) 4; 2/2 = 3/3
     2) 4; 1/2 = 2/4
  b. 8; 1/2 = 3/6

Page 159

The power of the indirect proof lies both in its simplicity of concept and in its ability to prove statements for which a convenient direct proof cannot be found. The example in the students' text does not represent the kind of problem for which an indirect proof is most effective, for the problem there can be more easily proved with a direct proof. (Direct proof: By definition of a proportion, both ratios must be equal. Since one ratio has a value of 1, the other ratio must also have a value of 1.) However, the example does illustrate simply and clearly how an indirect proof works. Here is another simple example you might like to use with your class.

  Example
    Problem: Prove that $12/3 \neq 6$.
    (Indirect) Proof: Suppose $12/3 = 6$. Then (because division is defined as the inverse of multiplication) $6 \times 3 = 12$. But $6 \times 3 \neq 12$ (because $6 \times 3 = 18$, and by definition a multiplication answer is unique), so we have a contradiction. Therefore, our supposition must be wrong, and so $12/3 \neq 6$.

Ask the class, "What if no contradiction is found? Does that prove the supposition true?" (The answer is no. Maybe we're just not bright enough to find the contradiction.)

A contradiction isn't always inevitable, for a statement assumed to be true may not necessarily be true at all. One of the most notable examples of this was discovered early in the 18th century when Girolamo Saccheri, an Italian Jesuit priest, set out to vindicate Euclid.

A popular belief at that time said that the postulate, "Through a given point not on a line, exactly one line is parallel to the given line," was redundant, that it could be proved from Euclid's other postulates and, consequently, that Euclid had erred in postulating it. Attempts to prove this succeeded only when other postulates were used instead, so for these proofs Euclid's postulate might as well have been used in the first place.

The controversy went on—was the postulate necessary, or wasn't it? Saccheri, an extremely able logician who was convinced that it was indeed necessary, decided to use an indirect proof. He denied the postulate with the idea that the resulting geometry would have to be self-contradictory, but despite his excellent efforts, no contradiction evolved, and his treatise on his findings became, in fact, a foundation for non-Euclidean geometry.

Apparently, however, the implications of Saccheri's treatise weren't fully considered, for it wasn't until the next century that Lobachevky (1826) and Bolyai (1832) developed hyperbolic geometry (by postulating two lines instead of one line parallel to a given line) and Riemann (1854) developed elliptic geometry (by postulating no lines parallel to a given line).

ANSWER

280. Suppose the second ratio's terms are equal. Then that ratio is worth 1. But the first ratio isn't worth 1 (because its terms are unequal), and so the two ratios aren't equal and therefore aren't proportional. This contradicts what we're given, which means our supposition has to be wrong, and so the second ratio's terms have to be unequal.

Page 160

The theorem of parts a–b will be used in later proofs, so it would be a good idea to make sure the students understand it and can say it. The correct statement of the theorem includes the stipulation that the numerators are nonzero. This was omitted here because a condition stated at the start of this series of problems excluded zero as any term of a proportion used here.

For part c, most students know they are not allowed to divide by zero, but they seldom understand why. It might help to point out that division is defined in terms of multiplication and so any division answer has to be verifiable by multiplication. (For example, 12/3 = 4 because 4 × 3 = 12.) Therefore, if there is any "division" problem that is not verifiable by multiplication, then that kind of division is not defined. This is the case for division by 0, because for 12/0 = ?, whatever we replace ? with will give us ? × 0 = 0, not ? × 0 = 12. So the reason that division by zero is not allowed is because it is not defined. Read on, however.

For 0/0, we have a different situation. Here, any answer we get is verifiable by multiplication. For example, 0/0 = 4 since 4 × 0 = 0; and 0/0 = 87.315 because 87.315 × 0 = 0. The problem, however, is

that all arithmetic operations are defined to have unique answers, but 0/0 has an infinite number of answers rather than a unique one. We see that for this case, too, division by 0 is not defined.

ANSWERS

281. a–b. The students' "proofs" may be something like this: a proportion says the two ratios are equal. You can't have something like 2/3 = 2/5, or 2/4 = 3/4 because they aren't equal, and the same thing would be true no matter what numbers you used.

However, the difficulty level of the problem was based on the assumption that the students would be expected to produce something similar to this:

a. Multiply both sides of the proportion by the product of the denominators. Divide both sides by a numerator. Reduce as far as possible. The result says the denominators are equal.

b. Multiply both sides by a denominator and reduce as far as possible. The result says the numerators are equal.

c. Division by zero is not defined, so we can never divide by zero.

Pages 161–2

ANSWERS

282. Use the product of the denominators as a common denominator, and convert the two ratios to ratios having this denominator. The denominators are now equal, so the numerators are equal (problem 281) and the problem is proved. (The left-hand numerator is the product of the extremes, and the right-hand numerator is the product of the means.)

283. One way to prove this is to list the 24 possible proportions, none of which will be a true statement.

Here is a shorter way: Since the product of 1 and any of the other three numbers will not equal the product of the remaining two numbers, we know from problem 282 that a proportion cannot be formed.

Page 163

Don't let your students reason that this problem can be proved by using problem 282 as evidence, for problem 282 is the converse of this one, and converses are not always true. For example, if something is a cat, then it is an animal; but it is not true that if something is an animal, then it is a cat.

This is not an especially hard problem for this level, once the students start thinking seriously about how to apply the hint given, and it is suggested that you don't give any hints about how to apply the hint. However, you might like to give them several examples (similar to the one in their text) to make sure they understand what the problem is claiming.

The problem doesn't ask for proof that the "extremes" pair and the "means" pair can be used in either order, or that any of the four given numbers can be used as the first term of the proportion. The students are quite likely to take for granted that these things are true, and it is probably a good idea at this point to let them make use of the concepts without pointing out that they are using unproved ideas. Since equality is symmetric and multiplication is commutative, however, the concepts are easily proved if the students do raise the questions.

ANSWER

284. We're given an equation having (a product of) two numbers on each side. Choose a number from the left-hand side, and divide both sides of the equation by this number. Reduce the left-hand side so that this number is eliminated. Do the same thing for a number from the right-hand side (choose, divide, reduce). The result is a proportion in which the given left-hand pair are the extremes, and the given right-hand pair are the means.

It doesn't matter which pair is chosen to be the extremes because equality is symmetric. That is, the proof above used the left-hand pair as the extremes, but we could have switched the sides of the equation so that the right-hand side became the left-hand side, and the proof would then have used the other pair as the extremes.

Pages 164–5

ANSWERS

285. Use problem 282 to get the product of one pair of numbers to = the product of another pairs of numbers. Then use problem 284 to arrange (a) the means and (b) the extremes in the other order.

286. Use problem 282 to get product extremes =

product of means. Then, using problem 284, choose the two numbers on the right-hand side (the old means) to be the extremes of a new proportion. Choose the old second term as the new first term, and choose the old first term as the new second term.

Page 166

The problem does not ask for proof of the students' "no" answers for question A, but you might like to ask the students for such proof.

ANSWERS

287. a. 1) No
      2) Yes. Problem 286 says we can invert both ratios.
    b. 1) No
      2) Yes. Equality is symmetric.
    c. 1) Yes
      2) Problem 285 says the extremes can be switched.
    d. 1) Yes
      2) Problem 285 says the means can be switched.
    e. 1) No
      2) Yes. Equality is symmetric. (Notice that this is the same problem as part b above.)
    f. 1) No
      2) Yes. Problem 286 says we can invert both ratios. (Notice that this is the same problem as part a above.)

Page 167

ANSWER

288. The students may come up with different answers for the different parts of the problem, but all answers can be the same: A proportion can be formed, so problem 282 guarantees that our four given numbers can be paired in such a way that the product of one pair = the product of the other pair. Choose any number for the first term of the proportion. Then (problem 284) the other number in that pair will be the fourth term, and the remaining two numbers will be the second and third terms (in either order).

Page 168

It is not enough to show an example here, for that

would show only one case for which the statement was true, whereas what is needed is a proof that the statement is *always* true.

ANSWER

289. The numbers are distinct, so there is a largest number and a smallest number. Use the largest number as the first term, and the smallest number as the second term, of the proportion. Then the quotient of these two numbers has to be larger than the quotient of the remaining two numbers, because these latter two numbers are closer together in size. Since the quotients are unequal, the ratios that indicate them are unequal, so the ratios are not proportional. One arrangement is to have the larger ratio's numbers before the smaller ratio's numbers. Another arrangement is to reverse this order.

Pages 169–71

ANSWERS

290. Once the proportion is formed, the two ratios can be inverted (problem 286), so the first term could have been the second term. Equality is symmetric, so the first term could have been the third term, and the second term could have been the fourth term. This shows that the first term could have been in any of the four positions. But from problem 288, any of the four numbers can be chosen as the first term, so it follows that any of the numbers can be chosen for any of the terms.

291. Note: Different examples may be given for the "yes" answers.
 a. Yes. $(1/2)/2 = 1/4$
 b. Yes. $(1/4)/(1/2) = 1/2$

292. a. Yes. $4/6 = 10/15$; three terms, but not the fourth, have 2 as a factor.
 b. Suppose a proportion is possible. Then it takes the form
  1st term/2nd term = 3rd term/4th term.
Multiply both sides by 2nd. Reduce the left-hand side, leaving only 1st, a whole number. Then the new right-hand side, too, must be a whole number, so 4th divides the product 2nd × 3rd. This is a contradiction, for 4th can't do this unless it is 1 or unless it has a factor in common with 2nd or 3rd, and we're given that neither of these is true. Therefore, the supposition has to be wrong, and so a proportion is not possible.

Page 172

This can be proved from scratch, but it's easier to use the theorems implicit in the proof of problem 288. To do this, however, it is convenient to use the contrapositives of the theorems, so you may have some groundwork to do with your class.

Give the students several examples of times they have used the contrapositive of a statement, instinctively knowing that the contrapositive was true because the statement was true:

- A teacher tells the class they're going to have a test, and the minimum passing score is 70%. The message given is, "If you're going to pass, then your score must be at least 70%." The students automatically know that if their score is not at least 70%, then they aren't going to pass.

- A youngster is assigned nightly dishwashing, an unloved task. Upset when told (s)he is too young to go skating with a group of friends, (s)he says, "If I'm old enough to do the dishes, then I'm old enough to go skating." Rephrased, this says, "If I'm not too young for the dishes, then I'm not too young to go skating," which is the contrapositive of what the youngster would really like to say, "If I'm too young to go skating, then I'm too young to do the dishes."

- Janine says the local vet doesn't seem to like animals very much, and Ricardo, who can't believe there's a vet alive who doesn't like animals, answers, "If he didn't like animals, he wouldn't be a vet," the contrapositive of, "If he's a vet, then he likes animals," or, "All vets like animals."

Toss in other examples of the everyday use of contrapositives as well so that the students realize how often such statements are used:

- If Bennetti weren't brave, she wouldn't be an astronaut ≡ If Bennetti is an astronaut, then she's brave.

- Nobody I know says things like that ≡ If it's anyone I know, then (s)he doesn't say things like that.

- If you can't say something nice, then keep quiet ≡ If you can't keep quiet, then (at least) say something nice.

- If Jankowski weren't an outstanding athlete, then he wouldn't be in the Olympic games ≡ If Jankowski is in the Olympic games, then he's an outstanding athlete.

- All mannerly people are polite ≡ All impolite people are unmannerly.

Next, help the students realize that a false statement has a false contrapositive:

- If someone eats junk food, then that person is fat ≡ If someone isn't fat, then that person doesn't eat junk food.

- If you like a class a lot, then you get terrific grades in it ≡ If you don't get terrific grades in a class, then you don't like it a lot.

- If a man has blue eyes, then he is a blond ≡ If a man isn't a blond, then he doesn't have blue eyes.

At this point, the students should recognize the contrapositive of an "if-then" statement and believe that a statement and its contrapositive can be freely exchanged for one another. Now help them transfer and apply their knowledge to mathematics:

- If two ratios are equal, then they are proportional ≡ If two ratios are not proportional, then they are not equal.

- If a fraction can be reduced, then it is not in its lowest terms ≡ If a fraction is in its lowest terms, then it cannot be reduced.

- If two numbers are equal, then all of their factors are common to both of them ≡ If not all of the factors of two numbers are common to both numbers, then the numbers are not equal.

Finally, ask the class for other examples of mathematical "if-then" statements, and ask that the contrapositives also be stated.

ANSWERS

293. See the proof of problem 288. In effect, these theorems are proved there:
   a. If a proportion can be formed from four given numbers, then any one of the numbers can be used as the first term.
   b. If a proportion can be formed from four given numbers, one of which has been chosen as a first term, then at least two of the three unchosen numbers can be used as the second term.

For this current problem, we'll use each theorem in its contrapositive form:
   a. Given four numbers, if one of them cannot be used as the first term of a proportion, then the four numbers cannot be the terms of a proportion.

   b. Given four numbers, of which one has been chosen to be the first term of a potential proportion, if at least two of the three unchosen numbers cannot be used as the second term, then no proportion can be formed from the four given numbers.

Statement (a) proves part b, and statement (b) proves part a.

For those students who think it's unfair to use as an authority something proved on the way to proving something else, when that "something proved" wasn't stated explicitly at the time, here is a proof (from scratch) of part a of the problem:

Suppose the problem's statement is false. Then all three of the remaining numbers must be tried as a second term before we can say for certain whether or not a proportion can be formed. If either of the first two (of the remaining three) numbers had worked, then we'd already know the answer. So neither of the first two numbers worked, and the supposition is that we could possibly get a proportion by using the last remaining number as a second term. But if this were true, then when we switched the proportion's means (permitted by problem 281) we'd get a proportion whose second term was one of the two numbers already rejected. This is a contradiction, so the supposition has to be wrong. Therefore, the problem's statement is true.

Page 173

ANSWERS

294. a. No. We've already tried and failed with 1st/

2nd $\overset{?}{=}$ 3rd/4th and with 1st/2nd $\overset{?}{=}$ 4th/3rd. Switching 1st and 2nd would merely result in inverting the would-be proportions already tried. Problem 286 guarantees that we can invert the ratios of a proportion, so if switching 1st and 2nd would give us proportion, then inverting both ratios of this proportion would also give us a proportion, contradicting our first two failures.

   b. 1) Yes; (no). Given the numbers 1, 2, 3, and 6, if we choose 1 and 6 for the first two terms, we won't get a proportion, but that certainly isn't enough to show that 1/2 = 3/6 isn't a proportion.

2) We quit trying because a proportion isn't possible; no. Problem 293 says we need try only two out of the three remaining numbers as the second term.

c. No. Problems 288 and 290 say that any number can be used as the first term if a proportion is possible.

Page 174

This is significantly harder than problem 247 in CRANIUM CRACKERS BOOK 2. For this version of the problem, we have to consider two things: students at this level, like those at the Book 2 level, still have difficulty realizing that if one number divides another, then all factors of the first number have to be factors of the second; the several cases to be considered (listed for the student as hint 2) demand complex thinking, including the ability to concentrate on the case being proved while at the same time considering what has already been proved and what is still to be proved.

ANSWER

295. Keep in mind that all terms are whole numbers. Use problem 282 to get

1st term $\times$ 4th term = 2nd term $\times$ 3rd term.

If one of the four terms, say 1st, is 1, then we simplify the equation to

4th = 2nd $\times$ 3rd,

thus showing that the two ordered pairs (4th, 2nd) and (4th, 3rd) have common factors (we're given, since 1st is 1, that neither 2nd nor 3rd is 1), and we are finished with the problem.

So suppose that none of the four terms are 1. Then we start again with

1st $\times$ 4th = 2nd $\times$ 3rd.

Divide both sides by one of the terms, say 2nd. This leaves the whole number 3rd on the right, so each factor of 2nd must also be a factor of either 1st or 4th (in order to have a whole number on the left, too). If 2nd divides a whole number of times into either 1st or 4th, then it has a factor in common with this term, and the other term has to have a factor in common with 3rd. If 2nd does not divide a whole number of times into either 1st or 4th, then it has a factor in common with each of them. In either case, we have two pairs of terms with a common factor, and we are through with the problem.

Page 175

A simple reference to problem 295 will not do for part b. The two pairs in problem 295 could be the two ratios of the proportion, which would not prove problem 296.

In effect, the indirect proof for part b establishes a contrapositive of the given problem: If two ratios are proportional, then either their four terms are not distinct or there is some factor that is common to at least one term of each ratio.

ANSWERS

296. a. Any counterexample will do—2/3 and 4/5, for instance.

b. Suppose the two ratios are proportional. Then (problem 282) 1st term $\times$ 4th term = 2nd term $\times$ 3rd term. Divide both sides by 1st, leaving the whole number 4th on the left-hand side. Then the right-hand side, too, must be a whole number, so each factor of 1st is also a factor of either 2nd or 3rd. We're given that 1st and 3rd have no common factors, so all factors of 1st are factors of 2nd. Analogously, by starting over and dividing both sides by 2nd, we determine that all factors of 2nd are factors of 1st. But the only time that all factors of one number are factors of another and vice versa is when the two numbers are equal, and this contradicts the given information that the four terms are distinct. Therefore, the initial supposition has to be wrong, and so the two ratios are not proportional.

Pages 176–7

ANSWERS

297. orlib, fanig, lemip, gromyx, cunir
298. a–b. yes
299. What is the area of a room eleven and a half feet by ten feet? (115 square feet)

Page 178

This is another Diophantine problem.

ANSWER

300. Of miscellaneous, toys, clothes, and transportation items, for $100 one could buy, respectively, 87, 6, 3, 4; or 75, 19, 4, 2; or 78, 11, 9, 2; or 81, 3, 14, 2; or 60, 40, 0, 0; or 63, 32, 5, 0; or 66, 24, 10, 0; or 69, 16, 15, 0; or 72, 8, 20, 0; or 75, 0, 25, 0.

Page 179

ANSWER

301. First weighing: Place all of one kind of ball on the scale, two in each pan. If the scale balances, then the odd ball is in the other set of balls. If the scale doesn't balance, the odd ball is in the current set of balls.

Second weighing: Choose the set that contains the odd ball. Put two balls aside and weigh the other two, one in each pan. If the scale balances, the odd ball is one of the two set aside. If the scale is unbalanced, then the odd ball is one of the two being weighed.

Third weighing: Choose the pair that contains the odd ball. Put one on the scale, and lay the other aside. Put one of the other two in the empty pan. If the scale balances, the odd ball is the one just now laid aside. If the scale doesn't balance, the odd ball is on the scale.

GLOSSARY

Words explained in the text are not listed here. To find the meaning of such a word, look in the Index for the page numbers where the word appears.

The definitions given here are as used in this book. See a dictionary for other definitions.

common factor—a factor that both of two numbers (or all of more than two numbers) have. (For example, 2 is a common factor of 6, 10, and 18. Three is not a common factor of 6, 10, and 18.)

contrapositive (of a statement "if P, then Q")—the result of exchanging and negating P and Q. (For example, given the statement, "If an animal is a tiger, then it has stripes," its contrapositive is, "If an animal doesn't have stripes, then it isn't a tiger.")

converse (of a statement "if P, then Q")—the result of exchanging P and Q. (For example, given the statement, "If an animal is a tiger, then it has stripes, its converse is, "If an animal has stripes, then it's a tiger.")

digit (dij uht)—one part, or component, of a written number. (For example, the digits of 637 are 6, 3, and 7.)

distinct (dis TING(K)T)—all different from each other. (For example, the numbers 2, 3, and 4 are distinct. The numbers in the set {4,5,4} are not distinct.)

factor of a number—a divisor (of the number) that leaves no remainder. (For example, 3 is a factor of 12, but 8 is not a factor of 12.)

power of a number—the value obtained by using only the number as a factor. (For example, $5 \times 5 = 25$ is the second power of 5. The third power of 6 is $6 \times 6 \times 6 = 216$.)

prime factor—a factor that is a prime number. (For example, 3 is a prime factor of 12. Six is not a prime factor of 12.)

prime number—a number other than 1 that has no factors except itself and 1. (For example, 2, 3, and 11 are prime numbers. Numbers 1, 4, and 6 are not prime numbers.)

significant (sig NIF ih cuhnt) digits—digits in an approximate number that indicate how exact the number is. An answer cannot have more significant digits than a number used to get the answer. (For example, $302 \times 1.8 = 543.6$. If 302 and 1.8 are both exact, then 543.6 is the answer. If 302 is approximate and 1.8 is exact, then 544 is the answer. If 302 is exact and 1.8 is approximate, or if both are approximate, then 540 is the answer.)

term—component or separate part. (For example, given the fraction $\frac{2}{3}$, its terms are 2 and 3; 2 is its first term, and 3 is its second term. Given a list of items, say

horse, bad-tempered old camel, baby elephant,

the list contains three terms, which are separated from each other by commas. The terms of a proportion are arranged like this:

$$\frac{\text{first term}}{\text{second term}} = \frac{\text{third term}}{\text{fourth term}} \text{.)}$$

INDEX

Alpha Centauri, 113. *Also see* Light-years.

Analogous. *Also see* Analogies, Analogy, reasoning by.

    reasoning, 71, 74, 75, 90, 93, 95

    relationships, 31–9

Analogies, Analogy

    definition, 47

    in proportions, 152–75

    just for fun problems, 42–6

    rearranging, 40–6

    reasoning by, 47–50

    standard form, 38–9

Answers and Comments, 183–213

Areas. *See* Miscellaneous problems.

Attributes

    finding common, 29

    identifying the outsider, 30

Balls. *See* Weighing balls.

Base. *Also see* Other bases.

    definition, 91

Clock arithmetic, 69–82

    24-hour clock, 77, 80–2

    A.M., P.M., 77–80

Contradiction. *See* Counterexample; Indirect proof.

Counterexample, 8–16, 73–4

    definition, 8

CrossNumber™ Puzzles, 17–21

Definitions. *See specific words.*

Diophantine problems, 67, 129, 148, 178

Directions. *See* Following directions.

Drawing inferences

    Humpty Dumpty, 22–3

    Little Jack Horner, 24

    miscellaneous problems, 7, 25–6, 63, 85, 118, 142, 147, 149, 176

Fairy tales. *See* Drawing inferences.

Fantasy, 3–6

Following directions, 62, 117

Fractions. *See* Ratios.

Glossary, 215–6

Great–aunt Martha. *See* Math Mind Benders®.

Grid problems. *See these categories:* CrossNumber™ Puzzles; Math Mind Benders®; Mind Benders®; Puzzles.

Identifying synonyms, 27–8

Index of refraction, 115. *Also see* Light-year; Speed of light.

Indirect proof, 159–175

Inferences. *See* Drawing inferences.

Letters, replacing with numbers, 134

Liars. *See* Truth-tellers and liars.

Light-year, 111–4

    definition, 111

Math Mind Benders®, 123–8

Measuring water. *See* Water jugs problems.

Messages. *See* Puzzles.

Middig, 15–6

Mind Benders®, 138–41. *Also see* Math Mind Benders®.

Miscellaneous problems, 64–5, 86–8, 99, 119–22, 132–3, 135, 137, 143–6, 150

    areas, 87

    belt around equator, 145

    bicycle, 86

    hairs on head, 144

    Norwegian goat, 135

    postage stamps, 146

    rainfall, snowfall, 143

    rocket ship, 99

    think of a number, 120

Number patterns, 108–10

Nursery rhymes. *See* Drawing inferences.

Odd balls. *See* Weighing balls.

Operations. *See* Operators.

Operators, 51–61

    definition, 51

    order of precedence, 51–61

Opposite. *See* Indirect proof.

Order of precedence. *See* Operators.

Other bases, 89–97

Patterns. *See* Number patterns.

Place values. *See* Other bases.

Precedence, order of. *See* Operators.

Problems. *See specific category.*

Proof

    indirect. *See* Indirect proof.

    problems. *See* Proportions, proof problems.

Proportions, 152–75. *Also see* Ratios.

    analogies in, 152–75

    definition, 152

    extremes and means, 161–4

    hints for proof problems, 156

    means and extremes, 161–4

    proof problems, 157–75

    terms of, 158, 161–2, 166–70, 172–5. *Also see* Glossary.

Proxima Centauri. *See* Alpha Centauri.

Puzzles. *Also see specific category.*

    rearrange letters, 66, 83, 98, 116, 136, 177

Ratios, 152–75, 157, 159, 165, 175. *Also see* Proportions.

    definition, 152

Refraction. *See* Index of refraction.

Relevant

    definition, 101

    information, 101–7

Significant digits, 111

Speed of light, 111–5

Supposition. *See* Indirect proof.

Synonyms, identifying, 27–8

Teaching Suggestions and Answers, 181–213

Transitivity problems, 118, 142, 176

Truth-tellers and liars, 1–2

Water jugs problems, 68, 84, 130–1, 151

Weighing balls, 100, 179

Zoffer, 15–6